Survival of the Fittest, the Fastest, and the Best: Praise for
JEFF AND MARC SLUTSKY

"Well, it looks like Jeff Slutsky is giving away money again. Every time I read one of those Slutsky Brothers books, I get so many new marketing ideas that it raises our company profits. It doesn't matter what profession you are in, this book is your best protection against personal or economic recession. Buy it and use it today."
—**Danielle Kennedy, author of**
Selling: The Danielle Kennedy Way,
How to List and Sell Real Estate, **and**
Super Natural Selling for Everyday People

∎∎

"Slutsky's low-cost gimmicks help drum up big business."
—*USA Today*

∎∎

"A 'Mercantile Marauder' who uses his wits to give small business an edge."
—*Chicago Tribune*

∎∎

"GREAT!"
—Joe Girard, author of *How to Sell Anything to Anybody*

∎∎

more . . .

HOW TO GET CLIENTS

JEFF SLUTSKY

with Marc Slutsky

WARNER BOOKS

A Time Warner Company

For Amanda

Warner Books, Inc., 1271 Avenue of the Americas, New York, NY 10020

Visit our Web site at http://warnerbooks.com

Ⓦ A Time Warner Company

Printed in the United States of America

First printing: September 1992

10 9 8

Library of Congress Cataloging-in-Publication Data

Slutsky, Jeff. 1956–
 How to get clients / by Jeff Slutsky with Marc Slutsky.
  p. cm.
 Includes bibliographical references.
 ISBN 0-446-39315-0
 1. Marketing. 2. Customer service. 3. Professions—Marketing.
 4. Public relations. I. Slutsky, Marc. II. Title.
HF5415.S57 1992
658.8—dc20   91-20155
                                                              CIP

Cover design by Michèle Brinson
Book design by H. Roberts

ATTENTION: SCHOOLS AND CORPORATIONS
WARNER books are available at quantity
discounts with bulk purchase for educational,
business, or sales promotional use. For
information, please write to: SPECIAL SALES
DEPARTMENT, WARNER BOOKS, 1271 AVENUE
OF THE AMERICAS, NEW YORK, N.Y. 10020

Acknowledgments

I'd like to thank the many people who made this book possible. To Jeff Herman, a great literary agent and good friend. Without his ideas and guidance this book would have been impossible. To Angie Christman for her hours of research. To my writing and speaking friends for their contributions and support and especially Bob Shook, Michael LeBoeuf, George Walther, Dorothy Leeds, Gene Hameroff, Bill Bishop, and Susan RoAne for letting me hock and drey. I'd also like to thank my staff and family for their support during this project: Don, Heide, Mom, Edye, Howard, Rick, Lisa, Paul, and Eileen. Lastly I'd like to thank my clients. You are the reason I write.

Acknowledgments

Contents

Introduction

How to Get Clients is a unique and complete marketing guide specifically written to help you develop a larger and more profitable client base. Most professionals are highly trained and expert in their field, yet have little marketing expertise in the complex and confusing area of selling services to new prospective buyers. Aside from providing expert services for clients, the ability to bring in new clients is paramount to a professional's success. There are hundreds of thousands of professionals in numerous areas that have to get more clients to pay higher fees for their services if they are to survive in the competitive times ahead.

The service economy is increasingly more competitive. As a result, large companies are restructuring, merging, and consolidating, leaving hundreds of thousands of highly skilled professionals to fend for themselves. At the same time, those remaining in these "leaner" and "meaner" organizations are under increasing pressure to bring in the business.

Is This Book for You?

This book is geared to professionals and business people who have gone out on their own or are given the responsibility of client acquisition in their present organization. It is also must reading for any ambitious corporate person who wants to climb the corporate ladder in a service organization because, while any trained professional can do the work for clients, it's the partners and future partners who actually bring the clients into the firm.

In an issue of *BusinessWeek*, an article entitled "For Law Firms, It's Dog v. Dog out There" stressed how the legal profession is becoming increasingly competitive.[1] A sidebar article, "The Latest Law Course: Marketing 101," stressed the need for sales and marketing:

> For the lawyers, it represents a bold new step into the world of competitive business. Traditionally they had shunned overt marketing efforts because of ethical restrictions and professional biases. But the rules have eased. In today's saturated legal market, firms are looking for every advantage they can find.[2]

Take a look at another profession where sales and marketing are just now becoming a major part of the practice. The first item of the "Business Bulletin" on the front page of *The Wall Street Journal* had the following:

[1]"For Law Firms, It's Dog v. Dog out There," by Michael Galen with Tim Smart, Geoff Smith, and Keith Hammonds. *BusinessWeek*, August 6, 1990. Legal Affairs section.
[2]"The Latest Law Course: Marketing 101," by Michael Galen. *BusinessWeek*, August 6, 1990, p. 58.

More lawsuits and the S&L crisis cause firms to take steps against exposure. The American Institute of CPAs tightens its membership rules. A national survey finds eight of 10 midsize accounting firms restrict services and 56% won't take clients considered "high-risk."[3]

This means that with fewer clients to choose from, accounting firms are becoming more aggressive in going after the business they do want. They also have to market expanded services. For the first time, sales and marketing are becoming a vital part of a successful CPA firm.

Another way to get clients is by merger and acquisition. Sam Schwartz, of Schwartz, Adelman, Kellerman & Marks, a midsize Ohio CPA firm, drastically increased his client base initially by buying other practices. In fact, Bob Kellerman merged his firm with theirs because it made sense for both. Merger and acquisitions is certainly a viable means of getting clients. It's a special area all by itself. Merger and acquisitions notwithstanding, marketing is the other way to get clients.

Must You Market to Thrive?

Everyone markets. You may not be aware of it, but every time you get a new client or expand services to an existing client, you've used marketing. It's really just a matter of the degree of aggressiveness to which you use it. This book explores the various *degrees* of marketing. If you need paying clients to pay the bills, you need this book.

Lawyers, doctors, and accountants are only a few of

---

[3]*The Wall Street Journal,* August 23, 1990, p. 1.

the examples given. These professions often require the most subtle marketing approaches. Most techniques that are successful in these professions are easily adaptable to other types of businesses. We also address industries where a more aggressive marketing stance is acceptable. Real estate, insurance, investments, and equipment sales are just a few more groups that also benefit from the information in this book.

It makes no difference whether it's a branch office of AT&T or IBM or a single consultant with a part-time secretary, *How to Get Clients* gives field-proven techniques needed to master the art of getting clients.

An Aggression Progression

This book is written in an "aggression progression." The earlier chapters provide you the most subtle marketing approaches. They get a little more aggressive and end with the most aggressive. Your particular situation dictates the degree of aggressiveness you wish to market. Whenever you market, you must be sensitive to possible backlash from others in your industry. Some may deem your approach unprofessional. It has to be balanced with the need you have for getting more clients. The balance is a personal preference. Take the ideas that are right for you and toss out the ones that aren't.

CHAPTER 1

Who Are Your Potential Clients and Why Do You Want Them?

It's difficult to be all things to all people and still have credibility. I realized this when I was asked, years ago, to participate in the Cancer Society's Bid for Bachelors. About twenty of us were auctioned off. We were to create and pay for this dream date. And of course, all the money went to charity.

I was up against some pretty stiff competition. There were a couple of pro football players and local celebrities. I decided to use a basic marketing technique of carving off a "market niche." From past personal experience it seemed like about a third of the women I had dated over the years had cats. And those who had cats were fanatical about their cats. So I created a date package geared specifically to cat lovers.

First my date and I would be picked up by a chauffeur-driven Cat-o-lac to be taken to the Columbus Zoo. There, in the Lion's Pavilion surrounded by exotic cats from around the world, we would have a candlelight dinner for two catered by a local restaurant called Katzingers. The centerpiece would be comprised mainly of cattails and pussy willows.

The limo would take us to the stage show *Cats*. On the way we would listen to music on tape from Cat Stevens, and my date would keep the tape as a memento of the evening. And just in case the evening would be too much, I had Dr. Myron Katz on standby at Grant Memorial to perform complimentary CAT scans. It was a cat lover's date come true.

I brought in the second largest bid for the evening. If you can't beat them with bulk, do it with brains. Mike Tomczak, former starting quarterback for the Chicago Bears, came in first.

Group Your Clients. The very first step in getting clients is to decide which clients you want to get. This is not as simple as it sounds. It's also more important than it sounds. Choosing your most appropriate client segment affects your growth potential, profitability, overhead, work load, and your general attitude and enjoyment of your work.

Why and How to Develop Client Segments

A "client segment" refers to the portion of potential clients that fit into a specific category. These segments are formed by using any criteria that you wish. Common criteria often used to form market segments involve demographic categories. These include age, sex, income, household size, marital status, buying habits, credit, and race. Client segments for businesses and organizations often are grouped by industry, sales or revenue, profit, number of employees, number of locations, products or services provided.

How to Focus in on Your Clients

Before you start seeking new clients, first look at your existing ones. There's an old sales and marketing adage called the "80/20 rule" that states, "You get 80 percent of your business from 20 percent of your clients." According to an article in *D&B Reports:*

> A small number of clients typically generates most of a business's sales and profits. Businesses must adopt key account marketing to ensure that big clients remain loyal and by ensuring quality client service. Key account marketing is based on adapting a business's internal requirements and decision making to client needs.
>
> To implement key account marketing, major clients must be interviewed to find out why they like doing business with a company. An annual review of key accounts' needs and requirements must be conducted. A company must play an active role in helping key clients get their quality standards. Companies also must take a proactive role and involve major clients in designing services or products improvements. They also must ensure that senior management takes a personal interest in major clients.[4]

Why the Ideal Client Is Ideal

To begin to understand where you might improve the quality of your client base, create different categories, then see into which ones your clients fall. Discover what they have in common and group them accordingly.

---

[4] "How to Keep Your Big Spenders Happy," by Mark Stevans. *D&B Reports* 30 (May/June 1990), p. 52.

Remember, the term *clients* can be used interchangeably with *customers, consumers, patients, patrons,* or *supporters.* "Clients" is any term you use to designate the buyer for your products and services. Your "ideal client" is probably one that falls into the top 20 percent of your clients that are responsible for 80 percent of your profit.

Joseph Sugarman, author of *Success Forces,* goes a step further with the 80/20 rule. He calls his version the "80/20/30 rule":

> I say that in business 20 percent of your profits create 80 percent of your headaches. For example, you might have ten clients, eight of which are just great but two of which create 80 percent of your problems. My rule says that if you sacrifice the 20 percent of your profits that create 80 percent of your headaches, you'll end up making 30 percent *more* profit.[5]

There are several elements you can look at to begin to develop these categories. The ones you would choose obviously depend on your type of business. Usually, your objectives guide your grouping process by the levels of profit and pain the client generates.

After going through your existing client base and placing each client in a few categories, you should begin to see a picture forming. The picture should give you an indication of where your clients come from. Or perhaps you'll discover which category of clients is more profitable or a reduced liability. You have to ask yourself, "If I could get more clients in any one of these categories, which ones would they be in and why?"

Identifying the most profitable segment of your client

---

[5]*Success Forces,* by Joseph Sugarman (Chicago: Contemporary Books, 1980), pp. 172–73.

base is critical to successful growth. This is reinforced in an article that appeared in *Industrial Marketing Management:*

> Diagnostic and prescriptive models were used to help understand sales profitability. The process helps 1) to assess the status of a client base; 2) to identify an *ideal* client base; and 3) to prescribe action that can help in forming the ideal client base. This model helps to bring structure to the assessment of the possible profit contribution of an entire client base.[6]

You should understand what makes a particular client profitable or unprofitable. By "profitable" we mean more than bottom-line net. The profile of your "ideal client" is based on the factors that are important to you. These may include: (1) length of term, (2) fee levels, and (3) required effort to service the client properly. You also have to consider whether a particular client "fits" into your business. Will serving this client move you closer to your goals, or does it take you in a less desirable direction? Does this client pose possible liabilities like moving you away from your strongest area of expertise?

To reach your long-term goals and build the type of business that you envision, you have to consider turning away the types of clients that don't fit the profile. This is not easy to do when bills are due and your staff insists on raises. According to an article in *American Salesman:*

> Eliminating small, unprofitable accounts allows professionals to spend time with better clients and

---

[6]"A Portfolio Approach to Account Profitability," by A. J. Dubinsky and T. N. Ingram. *Industrial Marketing Magazine* 13 (February 1984), pp. 33–41.

develop new business. [Professionals selling to new clients] should answer four key questions to rate accounts for their worthiness: 1) Does the client need the product [or service]? 2) Can the client use the product [or service] in quantities now or in the future? 3) Does the product [or service] meet the client's specifications? and 4) Can the client afford the product [or service]?[7]

To illustrate this, consider Bob Kramer, the owner of Kramer's Sew & Vac, a successful sewing machine dealership in the Cincinnati, Ohio, area. He carried both new and used machines. After analyzing his customer base he discovered something very interesting. Sales from the used machines contributed only 5.4 percent of his total profit, yet took up one third of his time and floor space.

Customers buying used machines were not of the same caliber as those buying the new ones. They might put down a very small amount of money and tie the machine up for as much as six months before final purchase. They seemed to live from paycheck to paycheck, unlike new-machine customers. So Kramer made the decision to stop selling used machines. He then allocated all the resources that went into the used machines to the more profitable new machines. With a small amount of effort and investment he instantly affected his gross sales and bottom-line profit.

Jinny Schulman is a very successful commercial real estate agent in Columbus, Ohio. In 1989 she completed a gutsy change in her business. She decided to work only with sellers, not buyers. Most agents work with both. The

---

[7]"Spotting Unprofitable Prospects" (Selling Techniques) (Sales Ideas That Work), by Ted Pollock. *American Salesman* 35 (March 1990), p. 23.

average agent spends much of his or her time with buyers in hopes of getting half of the commission on the sale. It's tough to give up a big portion of the potential business. But she identified this client segment as less profitable than the "seller" segment. It's a move that paid off big-time for Jinny:

> "It didn't make much sense to spend time with someone who has no commitment to buy from me. As a real estate agent I represent the seller. If I spend time with a buyer on properties other than those I list, then my focus is wrong. I spend 100 percent of my time representing those who have given me a six-month contract to sell what is usually their most important asset."

If a buyer is interested in properties other than those listed by Jinny, she refers the buyer to someone else. This approach is appreciated greatly by her clients. She reinforces her philosophy of working only for sellers when presenting to prospective listers. It sells the seller on her.

Furthermore, she won't buy properties she lists. Many commercial real estate agents buy the gems and spend much of their time on their own properties. Jinny's clients know that there is absolutely no conflict of interest. She concentrates on doing the best job for those that list with her.

An additional benefit from her disciplined focus on sellers is that the buyers are impressed with her during the transaction. When it comes time for them to sell, they often go to Jinny.

Creating Your Ideal Client Profile

To create the ideal client profile, it helps to develop a

"mission statement." Write down a paragraph, no more than four sentences, that describes what you do and the long-term goals you're trying to reach. These goals should be more on a philosophical plane, not financial. The money comes later.

For example, a psychologist with offices in the downtown area of a large city might write, "I provide patients the best quality help in dealing with the stress of working in upper-management positions of local businesses." This simple mission statement guides this psychologist in an area. She has attempted to carve off a certain market niche in this statement: "upper management of local businesses." This is both demographic and geographic.

When she first considered where to set up her practice, her mission statement guided her to downtown. This is the most convenient location for the "ideal clients" she wanted as patients. The downtown location also costs three times more than other areas. To target her ideal client base, it made sense nonetheless. The clients are willing to pay more for the convenience.

The mission statement we've chosen for our company, Streetfighter Marketing, is: "We teach businesses how to effectively market, promote, advertise, and generally increase sales using a shoestring budget." This identifies what we do and for whom. This also means that we *don't* do time management or leadership training. It means that we *don't* do media placement like advertising agencies. We stick only to the areas that give us a unique position in the marketplace.

When we were approached to write our third book, *Street Smart Tele-Selling: The 33 Secrets*, we had to ask ourselves, "Is a book on telephone sales techniques an appropriate area for us to expand into?" Before this we only taught local store marketing techniques to businesses.

These are promotional ideas that are executed by local managers on a neighborhood level. This is our forte and we've dominated this market segment. We've developed the telephone techniques as part of our own client acquisition program. This is how we get most of our clients.

On the other hand, when clients approach us to do seminars on team building, we referred them to our colleague, Mark Sanborn in Denver, a recognized expert in that area.

We then thought about our mission statement. Teleselling was a logical extension of our existing service. Telephone sales are needed by many of our clients and also expand our client base. Teleselling allowed us to offer more ideas to help clients reach the same goals more easily. Consequently, we wrote the book, produced the audio album, and developed the seminar.

Why Specialization Means Bigger Bucks

Our lives are becoming more and more complicated. The level of complication is growing. Despite the obvious negatives, this does mean opportunity. It's often difficult to be all things to all people. On an hourly, daily, or per job rate a "specialist" has the tendency to make much more than a "generalist." A key step in making this transition is to identify your unique market niche.

After you have examined your client base you need to examine other elements that help you identify your niche. To do this, answer these questions: What is it that you do most? Is that kind of work profitable? How profitable is it compared to other services you offer? What type of work do you most enjoy? Are you doing much of that type of work?

To illustrate the importance of identifying a market

niche, let's say you are unjustly accused of murder. It looks bad. The prosecutor is out to get you. You have a choice of three lawyers. We'll use fictional TV lawyers to help with this illustration. You can hire Arnie Becker from *L.A. Law*, Dan Fielding from *Night Court*, or Perry Mason. Now, keep in mind that Perry's fee is five times Arnie's and ten times Dan's. Your life is at risk. This is a murder case and Perry is a specialist. Similarly, if you wanted a divorce and your future ex was trying to take you for a ride, choosing Perry wouldn't make sense. Arnie is your man . . . unless you plan to take care of it by more drastic means.

The Three Big Advantages for Specialists

Client Perception. When a person has a problem he often thinks that his situation is unique and that handling the problem properly takes special care and expertise. In reality this may or may not be true. Still, the client perception is that it is true. The "perceived" value of your services is all that really matters when a client chooses the person to solve a problem.

Expertise Level. When you focus your business on a few specialized areas, you allow yourself the time and effort to master those particular areas. A generalist can't. No doubt your profession or business is becoming more complex and will continue to do so. By specializing you are making it easier on yourself to stay abreast of the latest developments in your specific area. You may not and probably could not do this in all the different services you provide as a generalist.

You can be a specialist and still provide full service to your clients. In larger organizations individuals have their own different specialties, but the whole of the organization provides the client with any service that may be required. In smaller groups you can ally yourself with other noncompetitive specialists.

Fee and Price Level. Tied directly to the expertise level is the fee level. A specialist is perceived as having more knowledge in a very specific narrow area. Consequently, most clients who have great need of this expertise are willing to pay a premium for it. Not only will they pay a premium but they will feel better about it. They feel they are getting a much greater "value" for their money than spending less money for similar expertise from a generalist.

Horizontal vs. Vertical Marketing

The computer retailer who markets to everyone and anyone within a five-mile radius from the store is selling in a *horizontal market*. A retail computer store like Computerland sells to a wide variety of clients primarily in a geographic area surrounding each of their locations. They don't specialize in serving clients in specific industries but rather focus on small or medium-sized businesses near their stores. Horizontal marketers are more likely to get the going rate for their standard computer equipment and off-the-shelf software. They sell the same stuff as other computer stores. Their products become a commodity. Price becomes one of the biggest issues in the buying decision. They are successful by offering a huge inventory of brand names at hundreds of convenient locations.

In contrast, VERSYSS™ is a vastly successful international *vertical marketer* of computers. Unlike a horizontal marketer, they market to several specific industries. According to Ken Ernstein, vice-president of marketing:

"What sets us apart from IBM, Digital Equipment, and the host of others is that we are specialists in our market segments. VERSYSS offers a total solution that incorporates computer hardware, software, installation, training, forms, and support. It's essentially one-stop shopping which we like to call 'single source' solutions. The four primary markets we target are construction, medical, materials management, and credit union. For instance, if you were a physician, VERSYSS software performs virtually every function needed in running a doctor's office such as billing, medical records, patient scheduling, and payroll. We are experts in a few market niches and do not try to be everything to everyone."

The vertical approach was discussed in *Marketing News:*

Microcomputer companies can reach broader, profitable markets by promoting industry-specific solutions instead of promoting only their technology. To successfully shift their marketing strategies, companies must do three things: 1) start specific market segments, 2) develop solutions to serve these markets, and 3) establish themselves in these markets by working through those elements that influence the clients.[8]

Both vertical and horizontal markets have their place. Yet the vertical markets provide a much more specialized service and can usually command a much higher price for their products and services. The client feels that buying from a specialist warrants the extra cost involved. Though

---

[8]"Computer Firms Must Reposition Themselves to Prosper," by Roberta Graves. *Marketing News* 22 (June 6, 1988) p. 7.

the price might be higher, the "value" received makes the higher price worth it to the buyer.

The Four Dangers of Being a Specialist

Danger #1: Too Narrow. When choosing a specialty or a few specialties, there is always a risk of creating a market that is *too* narrow. Make sure there is a big enough potential to make your specialization worth your while.

Silvan Krel is a CPA who has developed a good practice for himself over the years. He handles a variety of clients. One client happens to be a major insurance company offering disability insurance. They were starting to get what they thought were an alarming number of claims. They hired Silvan to review the financial situation of the claimants to see if they did, in fact, qualify for the disability payments.

This type of "forensic" accounting really intrigued Silvan. It was a great deal more fun than filling out individual tax returns. It was steady, profitable work and he is very good at it.

At first glance, it looks like an excellent opportunity to develop a lucrative specialty. Since there are likely more insurance companies in need of this expertise, it seems he could build an exceptional "vertical" market.

There were three problems. The first was that there were no other major insurance companies offering disability insurance in the area. There were very few within a reasonable driving distance. So, to dominate this market, it would require much travel.

Second, to dominate this market further, he would have to market aggressively. Insurance companies would have to be contacted. Information sent. Sales calls made. He hadn't yet developed a presence in this field. If he wished to pursue it, he would have to become the recognized expert.

Lastly, he would have to resign the bottom 20 to 30 percent of his least desirable clients to have the time to pursue this specialty further. That would mean a noticeable drop of revenue for a time. This is a difficult move for a sole practitioner like Silvan. He chose not to expand it at this time.

You must make these choices yourself. Is there a market or a couple of markets that you can dominate and make more lucrative than you could as a generalist? Does the risk outweigh the potential rewards? Are you willing to make the initial sacrifices needed to make this move? Tough questions.

Danger #2: Seasonal Swings. If the industry in which you've dominated has big seasonal swings, you may find that your business does too. To smooth out the peaks and valleys, you might look into specializing in a second or third industry with opposite seasons. On the other hand, you may like the idea of having an off season. It gives you the opportunity to work on your golf game, take a vacation, or clean the basement.

Danger #3: Cyclical Swings. Specializing in industries with big downturns can pose even more of a danger than seasonal industries. You usually don't know when you're headed into a major downturn or how long it's going to last. The solution is similar to seasonal businesses. Choose other specialties that have opposite cycles.

Danger #4: Geographical Disadvantage. Since you're going after a vertical market, you may have to expand your geographical territory to have enough clients in your "demographic" territory. So, though you may be getting higher fees and prices, you may have to do some extra traveling to work with your targeted client base.

You also may need to consider where you have to

locate your business. Certain types of specialists need to be located "where the action is." A free-lance copywriter, graphic artist, or commercial photographer specializing in national and regional advertising needs to locate near the clients. Most major ad agencies are in New York and Chicago. If they choose not to locate there, they need to plan on traveling.

Schwartz, Adelman, Kellerman & Marks, the medium-sized Ohio CPA firm mentioned in the Introduction, chose to locate their firm out of the downtown area. The national accounting firms all have offices downtown. Many clients have told the partners they don't like going downtown.

How and Why to Conduct Your Internal Capabilities Audit

Determining your specialties with the most potential for you begins with a simple internal capabilities audit. This helps you better understand your strengths and weaknesses. By playing to your strengths and avoiding weaknesses, you'll put yourself in a stronger competitive position.

It helps if you develop some simple guidelines for your client acquisition program. These guidelines tell you when to go forward and when to *avoid* a client. Developing ways to identify "red flags" or potential trouble areas is critical at this stage. You do this before you invest too much time or money in getting the client. A few red flags might include:

1. Promptness of payments
2. Turnover
3. Unrealistic expectations
4. Price/fee resistance

5. Unreasonable concessions
6. Excessive demands

There are three main areas you want to examine to figure out your opportunities of increased growth. They are:

1. Your client or market focus
2. Your expertise or unique talents
3. The Agony/Ecstasy Index

CLIENT OR MARKET FOCUS

Looking at your current list of clients, decide the categories in which they fall. You can place a client in more than one category if it makes sense. You're looking for patterns or elements that they have in common. Start with these three categories:

Revenue. Your first set of categories is revenue. Divide your client list into three different revenue ranges. You can base it on annual revenue or accumulated revenue to date.

Return on Investment. This category concerns itself more with profitability. Based on the amount of work you have to do to earn the revenue, place your clients into three category ranges: high, middle, low.

Product or Service Bought. Create categories for each major type of service and product line you offer. Keep it simple to begin with and you can break it down more later if you wish.

Now cross-reference the categories. Look at the top third of each category and see if there is a common thread. Does the most profitable work you do generate the most revenue? Oftentimes we seek clients based on what they spend, not necessarily on what we keep.

Look at the bottom categories. What products or services do you provide generating the least amount of revenue and profit? What would happen if you discontinued it?

YOUR EXPERTISE OR UNIQUE TALENTS

Make a list of areas in which you feel you are an expert or have some natural talent. Once you do this ask yourself if there are areas in your field that could also benefit from your special expertise or unique talents. An accountant whose family owned a small grocery store might have an advantage representing clients in the food industry. A doctor who also played high school or college sports might consider specializing in sports medicine. When you focus on areas in which you are very good or enjoy you're more likely to do a better job and thus command higher fees.

THE AGONY/ECSTASY INDEX

Gene Hameroff retired to Florida as chairman emeritus of one of the largest and most successful advertising agencies in Ohio. To keep busy between golf games, he started a consulting practice. Soon he became so busy consulting he didn't have time to play golf. He had a dilemma.

We sat and talked about his situation. First we looked at his list of clients. They fell into two main categories. The first was small advertising agencies. The second group was businesses that needed advertising. Through our conversation he expressed his frustration and even guilt about turning away business. He remembered very vividly what a struggle it was in the early years getting his ad agency off the ground.

It turned out that the companies that wanted him to help with their advertising were very demanding of his time. Furthermore, he didn't enjoy them. On the other hand, the small and medium advertising agencies were fun for him. In a one-day visit he could get them back on the right track. He'd leave a hero. After all, any mistake that they could make he already made and found a solution. He really enjoyed it and got paid a nice fee for doing it.

Now he simply refers the companies seeking advertising to some of his advertising agency clients. He stays with the work he enjoys and allows himself plenty of time to play golf in his "semi-retirement."

Some work is fun. Some isn't. Factor the ecstasy and the agony of the work you do into the equation. The more enjoyable the work you do, the better you'll do.

How to Expand a Narrow Client Segment

Eileen Oppenheimer is a creative marketer for an exclusive jewelry store specializing in very fashionable products like Piaget, Cartier, and Baum Mercier. The store is located in the nearest major city to a Japanese factory. Eileen noticed that some of the store's better clientele were Japanese. They barely spoke English, and Eileen (or Irene as her Japanese customers call her) spoke no Japanese. Yet they were great customers. They knew what they wanted and bought nothing but the best.

It seemed to make sense that there might be more potential Japanese clients out there. Eileen got a list of the upper-management Japanese who worked at the plant and other related industries. There were about thirty on the list.

Then she drafted a letter to be sent to the Japanese executives announcing the addition of Tiffany & Co. to the jewelry store's already prestigious lines and invited them to make an appointment. As it turned out, Eileen's son-in-law, a very creative advertising person in his own right, had taken a little Japanese in college, so to get the executives' attention, the letter opened up with a standard Japanese greeting, *"Ohayo Gozaimasu"* ("Good morning, how are you?") printed in Japanese characters. This also appeared on the bottom left of the envelope.

Eileen then had her suppliers turning their companies upside down for catalogs and point-of-purchase material in Japanese. She learned a few Japanese phrases and even arranged to have an interpreter on standby if needed.

The success of this very simple campaign was due to the following steps:

1. *Identify a narrow market segment.* Identify a very specific, and very profitable, segment of the client base.
2. *Find appropriate media.* Figure out the avenues (media) available for reaching that particular client segment effectively and efficiently (i.e., mail/ telephone list, special publications, meetings or events, etc.).
3. *Develop an appropriate message.* Develop a method to use the available media in a way that will get results, be cost-effective, and not jeopardize your level of professionalism and market position.
4. *Follow-up analysis.* Analyze the results of your effort. If successful, look for ways to make it more successful in the future. Also look for ways to apply the idea to other potentially profitable client segments. If not successful, try to figure out which elements fell short and how your effort could be improved.

Carving out a Niche. Carving out a market niche helps you appeal to specific segments. A Minnesota Super Value supermarket owner discovered that a number of Russian immigrants had moved into the market area. They had three different supermarkets from which to choose. He didn't like the odds. So he hired some children of the Russian immigrants to work in the store as cashiers and bag persons, and then had them create handmade signs to translate the point-of-purchase displays and specials into Russian. With little effort and expense he totally dominated this market segment by addressing the Russian families' unique needs.

You may gain several market segments over time. Once you've dominated a specific group and your competition finds it difficult to move in on that market segment, you can consider expansion. But you have to be careful. Expansion is dangerous because that's often when one has the tendency to let one's guard down on the "bread and butter" segment. Be careful. Expand carefully but protect your "flank" by making sure you're still dominating your key market segments.

When Expanding Your Services and Products Makes Sense

It may make sense for you to take the complete opposite approach. Does it make sense for you to expand what you offer your clients? Sometimes it does. This is a very tough call because you want to make sure that offering this new service or product doesn't interfere with your main business. This can be a costly mistake. It also can be a way to get an edge over your competition and create new profit centers from existing clients.

Here are a few questions to ask before considering an expansion of your products or services:

1. How much will additional inventory cost to get started?
2. How much extra training will my people need?
3. How much extra time will it take to carry the new line?
4. How much will this extra time keep us from other profitable areas?
5. How much do my existing clients want this new line?
6. What is the risk? If it totally bombs, what do I stand to lose?
7. What is the potential? (Figure potential in three ways: optimistic, realistic, and pessimistic.)

Lynn C. Fritz, of Fritz Companies, Inc., has had a 16.7 percent yearly increase in sales volume over the past five years. He expanded his father's customs brokerage company into a powerhouse in transportation and documentation for importers and exporters:

We took on *attendant* services to what we were doing. If the customer says to you, "Can you do this too?" and you say "Yeah!" If we were doing documentation to receive goods at ocean port in or out, that meant we were already handling most of the logistics and legwork for insurance claims. Why don't we write the insurance, too? You expand in such a way that you don't extend your personnel too far beyond what they're doing already.[9]

---

[9]From an interview with *Success Magazine*, "Relentless Growth," April 1991, p. 14.

Why Some Clients Talk a Big Game and Waste Your Time

There is one red flag mentioned earlier that deserves a little more elaboration. Client avoidance is critical when you discover that those clients have hidden money problems. They seem to sell you more than you might be selling them. There are usually reasons for this and not all of them are good. Be careful.

The "wait till the check clears" type of client wants you to be happy for as long as possible. They build you up. They're demanding but they love the work you do. Everything has to be done yesterday but they love you . . . until the invoice becomes past due.

You really have to be careful. They'll have many good reasons why you haven't been paid. They may even make some partial payments to keep you partially happy. They want you to continue to work. Once the bill gets to a certain level, you start talking to them more about payment than about their problem. That's when they stop returning your phone calls. Once you finally get hold of them, they become very honest about their financial situation . . . they're broke. (Even though they still drive around in a $50,000 car and live in a $500,000 house.)

It's at this point in the relationship they start complaining about the quality of your work. Everything you did was worthless. Elements in your agreement with them, which you thought were concrete and clear, become foggy and open to interpretation. You are now in a no-win situation.

Best-case scenario is that you may get fifty cents on the dollar after a long legal battle. Worst case is you get nothing. And in either case you will have expended much time and effort into getting this problem resolved. Not only does it take your time, but emotionally it zaps you as well. Nobody likes to be taken advantage of. You may spend more than it's worth just to make this guy's life miserable.

Solution:
1. Do a thorough credit check before doing any major amount of work for a client.
2. Find out who else has done work in the past for this client and call them. If there is a problem, often they'll let you know.
3. If possible, require a deposit or prepayment of fees.
4. If they refuse to prepay in any way, you have a tough decision to make. If it is a major corporation or government agency, you may have to follow their policies if you want the work. On the other hand, when working with smaller companies, be careful. You may want to consider walking away from a client if you have a gut feeling that you might get stiffed.
5. Use a binding contract. Have your attorney create a document that makes it very clear what happens in each contingency. Hint: If it comes back from your client with a bunch of clauses crossed out . . . beware.
6. Once payments become late, stop incurring additional expenses.

Use your best judgment with these clients. If you really need the work, it may be worth taking a risk. Just be aware of the risk you are taking and do what you have to do to protect yourself. And when you're negotiating the fee or price, make sure you consider the Agony/Ecstasy Index.

When offering volume discounts for time or products, charge full price for the beginning. Allow the discount on the rear end of the deal. In this way, if a client cancels, you're protected. They may only do a portion of what you agreed to. Though you base your price on a specific volume, the client still looks at the discounted price. Then you have the makings of an angry disagreement. Be careful.

Five Action Steps to Take Now

1. Review your existing clients and place them in categories. Identify what they have in common.

2. Look for client segments that are less profitable. Phase out the smallest one. Now.

3. Use the extra time from the phase-out to go after more clients in your most profitable category.

4. Look at your operation and identify those products or services that are unique, profitable, and fun (or at least less tedious). Begin now to specialize more in those areas.

5. Begin to assemble a plan to promote your specialized areas to the profitable client segments you want. The remainder of this book helps you to that end. Good luck.

CHAPTER 2

How to Establish Credibility so Clients Take Notice

Clients hire based on credibility. Your actual expertise is irrelevant. Getting the client's commitment directly relates to your ability to *prove* your credibility. Your prospective client must believe that you possess the skill to solve his or her problems or exploit his opportunities before he or she will hire you. We will assume that you already have this skill. The goal of this chapter is to show you how to identify and demonstrate those elements that convince clients of your credibility.

First you need a marketing definition of "credibility." A quick glance at a thesaurus gives us: honesty, trustworthiness, integrity, reliability, and believability. It almost sounds like a Boy Scout pledge. When a client is considering hiring you for his or her special needs, he or she is taking a risk. There is usually no guarantee that you will provide the desired result. *You* may have no doubts, but it's your clients who are making the decisions.

Without the proper illustration of credibility it is

extremely difficult to convince a client not only to hire you but to understand the merit of your price. Using a variety of credibility builders together seems to have impact way beyond the value of these techniques individually. The following synopsis of an article written for accountants hits the nail right on the head.

> The accountant in private practice needs to develop marketing skills. Strategies should be developed to promote oneself and the practice. Attendance at professional meetings helps to develop contacts. Offering oneself as a public speaker where clients may meet provides much exposure. Taking or giving seminars provides exposure. Press contacts are invaluable. Writing articles in publications that clients may read is very good advertising, as are books. Desktop publishing now makes newsletters a cottage industry; allows self-promotion while simultaneously supplying the reader with information.[10]

Nine Areas for Increasing Your Credibility Visibility

Though written for accountants, the ideas expressed above are adaptable to just about any type of business or profession. This article notwithstanding, here are nine areas for demonstrating credibility:

1. Credentials
2. Testimonials
3. Positive publicity
4. Writing and publishing newsletters

---

[10]"Strategies for Marketing Your Accounting Practice," by Robert E. Hieghtchew, Jr. *The CPA Journal* 57 (September 1987), p. 84.

5. Writing and publishing articles
6. Writing and publishing books
7. Public speaking
8. Community involvement
9. A winning image

We'll look at each area as it relates to building credibility. Often these marketing ideas provide much more than credibility, such as creating exposure and client demand. The "how to" aspects and additional benefits of many of these ideas are addressed in step-by-step detail in later chapters. For now, however, we'll look at ways these ideas help you build credibility.

Credentials

Credentials are an important part of establishing your credibility. Professionals usually display their diplomas and awards in their office. This builds credibility, but there are other ways to increase drastically the level of credibility in the mind of your potential clients.

Most professionals are required to have certain credentials. An accountant needs state certification, a lawyer a J.D., a doctor an M.D., D.D.S., D.O., etc. Are there degrees or designations that give you more credibility in your area? A lawyer who specializes in medical malpractice and has an M.D. should have an edge over a lawyer who doesn't. A CPA who also has an M.B.A. might have a little more clout with certain business clients than other CPAs.

A Professional Designation. You don't go back to school just to get degrees. But if you have certain designations that help you gain an edge, by all means use them. As a professional speaker I've received the CSP

(Certified Speaking Professional) designation from the National Speakers Association. To qualify, speakers must meet many strict criteria. These include a minimum of 250 paid speaking engagements over five years, at least one hundred different clients, at least thirty hours of continuing education, and more. It's not an easy designation to get.

At this point, outside the National Speakers Association it doesn't really mean a whole lot. Still, it could give us a slight edge over another speaker under consideration. While probing the prospect we might ask, "Does this other speaker have a CSP designation?" When the meeting planner asks, "What's a CSP?" it gives us the opportunity to explain what it means and the advantages of using someone with that designation. Just being a member of the National Speakers Association might give us that edge if the other speaker isn't. The point is that there might be designations that you take for granted that could be molded into further developing your credibility.

Lead Us Not. There's a reverse side to this as well. There seems some temptation to use certain designations that aren't rightfully earned. It seems like it is just common sense not to claim what you are not. Unfortunately there have been too many cases of someone falsely claiming a Ph.D. or another designation. And when they get caught, the damage is often irreversible. Very successful careers have been destroyed when a false claim was discovered. It's not worth the risk. Enough said.

Awards. Don't discount awards, special recognition, or certifications given by your company or association that could help build your credibility. You may not think that the award is anything special, but anytime you're honored it might impress a client.

Client Testimonials

Third-party testimonials from satisfied clients are a most effective way to help a potential client feel better about using your products and services. Plus they cost nothing. A prospective client is more at ease knowing that others have been pleased with your work.

You use these testimonials in different ways including:

1. As part of requested information after meeting or talking to a prospect
2. As part of a proposal or presentation portfolio that a client takes with him
3. Support material in a conference or waiting area
4. The first meeting where a presentation manual is used in helping clients clearly understand what unique benefits you offer

Testimonial Letter. A letter, on client letterhead, is the easiest way to present your past successes. A client simply writes you a thank-you letter in appreciation for the fine job you did. Client testimonial letters come in any length and can say just about anything. The ideal result of prospective clients reading these letters is that they feel really good about using you.

Besides testimonial letters from satisfied clients, you can also use letters from other sources. These include peers, trade organizations, celebrities or politicians, and community organizations.

Your Peers. Having letters from your peers in your industry is a good way to start building credibility. The greater the status of the peer, the better it is for you. Though the peer's name may be meaningless to your client, the title held isn't. When your contemporaries endorse you, it helps increase a potential client's comfort level.

Celebrity Endorsement. Associating yourself with these groups helps impress upon your prospective clients that you are special. In the right circumstances, letters, photos, and autographs from celebrities help set you apart from your competition. Ron Dentinger is a speaker and comedy writer who has written for, among others, Henny Youngman. Ron knew that Henny was in advertising before he became a comedian, so Ron told Henny about my book *Streetfighting*. One day I got a letter from Ron with a photocopy of a letter Henny wrote to Ron. In his note he said that next time Ron talked with me, he would like to get a copy of my book.

Of course I immediately mailed him an autographed copy. A few weeks later I got a handwritten letter from Henny Youngman on his "King of the One-Liners" stationery. He told me he really liked the book and learned a lot. He also invited me to have lunch with him at the Friars Club the next time I was in New York. A month later I'm having lunch with Henny Youngman. He was a funny and gracious host and it was a very enjoyable experience. We've become friends and my secretary got the biggest thrill when Henny called the office asking for me.

Henny's autographed picture and letter praising the book gives me a little more credibility when we're up against other speakers. We can only use this material when a client needs an entertaining keynote speech with humor. My association with Henny Youngman, in these situations, helps. (It also impressed all my relatives.)

Publicity Reprints

Another area that builds credibility is positive press. How to *get* publicity will be discussed in a later chapter.

For now, however, we'll explore ways to exploit the publicity once you've gotten it.

Most publicity is an article or interview in the news media. On the local level it might be an interview in your local newspaper or magazine. It could also be an interview on a radio or television broadcast. The exposure alone is good for getting leads and building credibility. The more positive the exposure, the better. Yet the benefits of this exposure are soon dissipated. You need to preserve it and incorporate it into your marketing effort.

Writing and Publishing

Writing and publishing are powerful ways of developing credibility because they help show that you're an authority on your subject. It also converts your authority into a tangible item that can be used in your marketing.

There are three types of writing and publishing helpful in enhancing your credibility: newsletters, articles in publications, and books.

The beauty about writing and getting published is that it is a very subtle way of gaining exposure and credibility. Many professions still frown on the more direct forms of advertising, yet admire published work. After all, if college professors must "publish or perish," then publishing should be dignified in your field.

Newsletters. Of the three approaches to publishing, a newsletter is the surest way to get exposure, since you have complete control over the publication. Newsletters allow you to stay in contact with your clients on a regular basis. Writing a newsletter can be an involved process, but with desktop publishing capabilities, it's possible to create a very professional-looking newsletter, very inexpensively.

Writing the newsletter is the more difficult aspect of it. Once you start publishing your newsletter, you must carry forward. But that regular contact with those on your mailing list allows you to stay utmost in their minds and in a very credible way.

Articles. Articles that you have written for various publications also give you tremendous credibility. Being published, whether in your local media or your trade media, reinforces to clients that you have a high level of expertise in your field.

An article published in your trade press is likely never going to be seen by potential clients. In fact, it is most likely to be read by your competition and vendors. There's nothing wrong with this provided you don't give them proprietary information in the article that can be used against you. You also have to be careful about letting potential competition know of your success. Others may decide that there's business there for them as well.

The next step is to explore writing a regular feature for that publication. The more times you appear in that publication, the more you'll get noticed. Frequency is a critical factor in marketing. Obviously the downside to a regular feature is that you have to come up with a new article regularly. If the opportunity is there, you'll have to ask yourself if it's worth it.

With such an opportunity think about the editor's note at the end of your article. The typical editor's note is something like: "Jeff Slutsky is a marketing consultant living in Columbus, Ohio." If possible, it's nice to have your company name, address, and phone number too. It may not be allowed but it's worth a shot.

The exposure and credibility from the article are well worth the effort. However, when first talking to the publication, you can sometimes negotiate free advertising space as compensation for writing the article.

Moreover, if you do write a regular feature, after a period you'll have a collection of articles. This is the beginning of your own book. This is the topic of the next section and brings up a point. *Make sure when you agree to write an article or series that you, not the publication, retain the rights.* This is very important if you wish to leverage your effort into a book or provide your articles for other publications.

CLIENTS PAY ATTENTION WHEN YOU WRITE "THE BOOK"

The single biggest credibility builder is writing a book on your area of expertise. Most people feel that a person who writes a book is the ultimate authority on a given subject. Often it's true. Despite realities, however, the perception is there. From a marketing standpoint, this is paramount.

It doesn't have to be a great book. The better it is, however, the better off you are. The problem with writing a book is that it is a major undertaking and it's often difficult to get published.

There are two ways to getting your book published. The first is have a publisher do it. For a first-time author this is not easy. It is worth the effort, though, since it is tremendously credible and you have no out-of-pocket expenses. Sometimes you might even get an advance against future royalty.

Your primary purpose for getting published, remember, is building credibility. So it's important to negotiate a few things in your contract toward this end. One critical issue is the price you pay for the books from the publisher. A typical author's discount is 40 percent off retail. Since your book has such an ability to promote your credibility, you want to be able to buy it at a rate that allows you to give them away to qualified potential clients. It is going to be your best brochure, whether they read it or not.

It may help to work through a literary agent when you're trying to get published. According to Jeff Herman, of the Jeff Herman Literary Agency in New York, and author of *The Insider's Guide to Editors, Publishers, and Literary Agents,* "the advantage of using a legitimate literary agent is it's your door opener. The agent gets you access to the powers that be and insures that at least your material is read."[11] The agent also has a good sense of what the publisher will allow during the negotiations.

The second way of getting published is to do it yourself. Self-publishing is becoming much easier with the arrival of desktop publishing. The big advantage of self-publishing is that you retain all the rights to your book. You have total control. You decide how the cover should look and for how much the book should sell. You even decide if it should be paper or hardcover or both. Perhaps the biggest advantage is that you buy the books at cost.

A publisher who retails your book for, let's say, twenty dollars a copy will charge you about twelve dollars direct. (That may vary from publisher to publisher.) On the other hand, if you publish yourself, after you've paid for setup you can buy a hardcover book for under four dollars and a paperback for under two. If you plan to buy a few thousand, that's a big savings.

When you self-publish, though, you have to pay for

---

[11]*The Insider's Guide to Publishers, Editors, and Literary Agents,* by Jeff Herman (New York: Pima/St. Martin's Press, 1991).

the initial setup. It has to be proofed and typeset and negatives and plates have to be made. The first copy may cost you many thousands of dollars. After that, though, you save a lot.

All things being equal, you're probably better off getting published and letting the publisher handle all the headaches. You'll also probably get some distribution and exposure that you would not have if you're self-published. One last thing you want to negotiate in your contract: If the publisher takes your book out of print, you want the rights back. Better yet, get them to agree to give you not only the rights but the negatives as well. In that way, if it's taken out of print, you'll pay a much smaller setup fee for republishing it. You can even redesign the cover so that it does a better job of selling you or your company.

Writing the Book. If you can't write, don't worry. There are plenty of ghostwriters available who can convert your thoughts to words and create a manuscript. Again, a good agent can help you do this.

If you can write, then do it. Make sure that your book is easy to read and understand. It doesn't have to be huge. Sometimes less is more, within reason. A book of 50,000 to 70,000 words is enough to be credible. (This book is about 67,000 words cover-to-cover.) If you have much information to share, you might see if it can be divided up into more than one book. Keep them wanting more.

Another problem that most people have when they begin to write their first book is that they want to create the perfect book to end all books on the subject. That notion keeps most people from ever writing their book. The best thing you can do is keep it simple. Don't be afraid to quote other sources—even competitors. The more sources you quote, the more credible you are. Ego often stands in the way, but think of it from your clients' point of view. All of it doesn't have to be original. But you do need to present the information in an original manner. Using outside sources enhances and enriches your book. It also adds more credibility. The ideas may be yours but they are reinforced by other experts.

In the Introduction of this book, I said that most of the ideas in this book aren't mine. We've interviewed many different people from many different industries. We've reviewed many books and articles. We've borrowed basic ideas from my first three books. But then we've adapted them to the goals of this book.

Leverage Your Book. One last thing about writing a book. Before it goes to press, whether self-published or not, find out how much it would cost to run extra covers. Once the cover is on the press for the book, it costs very little to run extra: perhaps seventy-five dollars per thousand, or only seven and a half cents apiece. This is a high-quality printing job on high-quality paper.

These overruns make powerful yet inexpensive brochures. With strong copy and a good design on the reverse side of the covers, you get a very high-quality, high-impact brochure at little cost.

Carl Hammerschlag, M.D., used a little twist on this idea when his book *The Dancing Healers*[12] was published in trade paperback. He got extra book covers and made inexpensive postcards by trimming off the backs. He uses them for informal correspondence and promotional programs. Very inexpensive, very high quality and high impact. Again, you'll be learning how to use these tools in greater detail in later chapters.

Once you have the book written, you have the option

---

[12]*The Dancing Healers*, by Carl A. Hammerschlag, M.D. (San Francisco: Harper & Row, 1988).

of selling (or giving) reprint or serial rights to magazines. This further creates demand for the book. If the magazine has no budget for the serial rights, offer to trade the rights for advertising space in the publication. It's better than just giving it away free. You might want to have an 8¼″ × 10¾″ camera-ready ad for your book created in advance. Now you can immediately seize these free opportunities when they arise. Have the ad prepared so you can send the publication a "film positive" or "velox." This is a photo-quality reproduction of the original ad.

You may even be able to work out an arrangement with the publication to sell the book for you. They buy wholesale or on consignment and make some profit selling it.

One last thing about books. Once you've been published, there are usually more opportunities for getting publicity. You might get book reviews and interviewed as an author. It goes back to ideas mentioned earlier about publicity.

Book signings at your local bookstore are yet one other way of getting extra leverage with your book. Even if self-published, books by local authors are of specific interest to the neighborhood bookseller.

How Public Speaking Puts You in Front

Public speaking is an excellent way of developing credibility as well as awareness and exposure for your business. There are many opportunities for providing speeches and seminars. These opportunities get you before your prospective clients. Like writing articles or a book, public speaking to the right group literally puts you on a pedestal. You are the expert, and many potential clients are giving their attention to you. It's now up to you to turn this opportunity into new clients.

You'll learn more of the mechanics and logistics of using public speaking as a promotional vehicle in later chapters. At this point you'll examine how public speaking can enhance your credibility.

There are usually three groups that you can provide speeches to: (1) your potential clients, (2) your peers, and (3) your community. The first group, potential clients, is obviously the most important group to speak to for getting business, but for building credibility the other two groups can help as well.

Speaking before one's peers brings a certain amount of prestige with it. Since your fellow practitioners are gathered to learn from you, your clients may view the event with significance. If given a choice, whom would you rather hire: the teacher or the student?

The least valuable group to speak to is your local community. It may be a group that needs a speaker and they're not too particular with who they get. Though not as valuable as the first two groups, this avenue gives you an opportunity to practice your presentation skills. Professional speakers hone their skills by giving the same or similar speeches often. They experiment with new anecdotes or humorous examples to illustrate points. Something happens in the audience and there's an ad-lib that worked great and can be incorporated into future presentations. The speech you gave five years ago is only a fraction as effective as the one you give today, though it's basically the same material. Pacing, timing, facial expressions, all get fine-tuned with experience.

It's always a good idea to try out new material on an audience that is not a primary group of potential clients. If the material bombs, it doesn't cost you anything. You're given another chance to make it work properly.

When Community Commitment Causes Client Calls

Community commitment can be a powerful way to gain credibility and at the same time help you to get exposure and make important contacts. "Community" can be looked at in two different ways. The first is the geographic community where you live and work. If you do most of your work in your city, this form of community involvement is worth consideration. The owner of a car dealership could benefit greatly by getting involved in the right cause in his or her community. The dealership's customers come from that community, and any exposure, goodwill, and credibility created by such an effort can translate into sales.

If you do most of your business nationally or internationally to a narrow market or "vertical" client segment, you have to redefine "community." In this situation your community is your industry or the related industries you serve. A free-lance photographer traveling the world for major news publications would gain little marketing advantage by doing a lot of hometown community service work. That's not to say that you shouldn't. If it is something you feel strongly about, by all means, contribute as you wish—just don't look at it as a marketing effort with an expected return on investment.

In this situation, the photographer might be more involved in associations, trade shows, and trade publications that cater to the major news groups. From a purely marketing point of view, exposure on this level could elevate the photographer's career.

How to Create a Winning Image

Creating a positive image is important to helping build your credibility. Image has to do with several different areas that vary in importance depending on the type of clients you wish to attract. Some areas for consideration include dress and grooming, promotional materials and letterhead, offices, car, entertainment, and affiliations.

According to Robert L. Shook, author of *Winning Images:*

> My philosophy has always been to dress in a somewhat conservative manner when conducting business so that I'd offend the least number of people. Since it is most important to have everything going for you in business, you cannot afford to wear clothes that might have an adverse effect on certain customers.[13]

Potential clients form an impression of you simply by your appearance at your first meeting. So you have to make sure that your appearance reinforces the image you wish to convey. When you meet a prospect for lunch, there are many elements that instantly create images in that one encounter. If your client base is upper management and executives, you don't want to skimp. At the same time you want to make sure that it doesn't look like you're going out of your way just to impress that person.

For example, you don't want to borrow or rent a Mercedes if you normally drive something else. Once a client discovers that the Mercedes was just there to impress, you destroy your credibility and it's nearly impossible to get it back. At the same time, you may have to make an important decision about your 1979 Impala

---

[13]*Winning Images,* by Robert L. Shook (New York: Macmillan Publishing Co., 1977), p. 17.

station wagon. If clients often see you in your car, it's important to consider a car that won't make you suspect. You should present success but not to excess.

Obviously you have to weigh the importance of these items and you certainly can't afford to go broke doing it. Common sense helps here. In my business, for example, it is very unlikely that our clients would ever see our offices, since our clients are located all over the country and we usually visit them. Therefore, it wasn't important for us to have expensive office space with plush decor in the downtown area. On the other hand, it was important that we have a good telephone system and quality promotional materials. We put much of our "image" resources into the quality of our letterhead, brochures, and promotional materials. This is how most of our clients form their opinion of us. The car I drive is not as important, since they don't see it.

What are the important elements for your operation? Do clients come to your offices? If so, you have to think about the image you wish to convey. Working out of your house, for example, might turn off certain types of clients. Then you must ask yourself if the clients that you're likely to turn off are the targeted group you want to go after.

Even if certain clients are informal in their environment, it is not necessarily an invitation for you to become informal too. Visiting a client at home, for example, you may find that the client is very informal. Yet you still need to dress conservatively. The client may never say a thing if you dress informally but may wonder about your credibility.

Once you sense it's proper, it may be fine for a man to remove his suit coat and perhaps even loosen his tie a bit. Sometimes the client may be more at ease if you do this. There are no strict rules. You need to develop a sixth sense about it. Yet, if you're going to err, do so on the side of conservatism. Better safe than sorry.

If you do much work in your car, you need to have a phone there too. Not having a car phone might cause the client to feel a little less comfortable with you. The client may never say so or even realize it on a conscience level. Giving your clients your mobile number and putting that number on your business cards will strengthen your client relationships.

Image aside, having a phone in your car is just good business sense. The time in your car is wasted. Though you're paying for the airtime to make calls in your car, it allows you to make use out of dead time. It's not the best way to conduct an initial phone call to a prospective client, but it is ideal for working with good long-term clients and taking care of operational details.

One good way to figure out what type of image you should portray is to observe your existing clients. Examine how they dress, accessorize, what they drive, the clubs they belong to, and the quality of their office decor. This gives you an indication, but you must be careful. You don't want to outdo your clients. They might feel threatened. This is not a contest but rather a way of breaking down possible negative barriers. It would be just as bad, for example, to drive a Rolls-Royce or a Ford Escort when your clients drive Jaguars and Mercedeses. Give it some careful thought.

If you're young, female, or a minority, you may have some difficulty working with certain types of clients. It's not fair but it's the real world, unfortunately. You have to be sensitive to potential clients' subconscious prejudice.

Such was the case when I first started in business for myself at twenty-four. I did several things to get over my clients' negative reaction to my youth that prompted me to write the following essay describing the situation:[14]

---

[14]Excerpted from "Confessions of a Streetfighter," ©1990 by Jeff Slutsky.

My dream is to look fifteen years older. I realize that may sound a little strange. My age has cost me a lot of money. I started my own company when I was twenty-three years old. To compound the situation, I'm 5'5" tall and for some reason, many business people equate credibility with age and even height.

Now, some eleven years later, I still look like I'm eighteen. On many occasions, as I fly around the country to present my Streetfighting program, some middle-aged business-looking person next to me on the plane strikes up a conversation that usually ends up with a question like, "So, what's your major?"

I have to admit, now that I'm in my mid-thirties and have built up some credentials, it's fun. It wasn't, however, in my earlier career when I was struggling to keep my business alive. My age and youthful appearance have definitely cost me a lot of money.

You would think with all this grief my age has caused that it would make me old before my time. No such luck.

The first painful experience with my age started after I was hired to help a large restaurant that had some very big problems. It was perhaps four months into the job and things were really moving along. My special marketing and advertising program which I affectionately refer to as Streetfighting was just starting to make headway.

To show his appreciation, my client, who very seldom took an active role in this business, asked me to join him for breakfast. I did. The waitress came over carrying two coffeepots and asked us if we wanted coffee. I asked for a diet soda. That's what I always drink for breakfast.

"Diet soda for breakfast. Are you kidding? Don't you drink coffee like normal people?" he asked with a pained look on his face.

I went on to explain that I never acquired a taste for coffee. I was raised in the coffee business. My parents had a coffee service and vending company and I'd make deliveries after school, pack coffee on weekends, and basically felt that coffee was ruining my social life. I hated coffee... wouldn't even eat coffee ice cream. I guess it was a form of teenage rebellion never to drink the stuff. Thank goodness they weren't sex therapists!

For some reason this disturbed him. He took a big sip of his fresh-brewed decaf, then asked the question that turned out to be my kiss of death: "By the way, Jeff, how old are you?"

At the time I really didn't think anything of it. Actually I was quite proud to have come as far as I had considering how young I was, and I responded without hesitation, "I'm twenty-three."

The man almost had a coronary on the spot. Here he had entrusted his multimillion-dollar operation to a mere child, and within the week, I lost my biggest account.

Needless to say, I was devastated, both emotionally and financially. I had lost a client, not because I didn't do my job right, but because I was too young. This was after he was getting results from my efforts.

Fortunately I recovered quickly. That's one thing I was good at. I realized that it was vital that I use some of my own marketing moxie to solve my credibility problem created by my age. So I took myself on as a client. This was important because when I work with a client, I always do it fanatically. I remember when I consulted Weight Watchers, I took an inch off my waist. After consulting with a Nautilus fitness center, I added an inch and a half to my biceps. And months after handling a disco, I learned to dance like John Travolta. I did, however, turn down a job from a health clinic in Los Angeles specializing in breast enlargements.

To get in the right frame of mind, I signed a contract with myself. I wrote myself a check . . . I didn't cash it, of course, because I knew better. And thus started a campaign to make Jeff look older.

The first thing I did was burn my green polyester leisure suit. Very flammable. Then I had to deal with my car. At the time, I was driving a 1969 Opel GT. This is a little two-seater German sports car in two shades of primer gray, faded orange, a ring of rust spots, and one headlamp that was stuck in the "up" position as if the car was winking. Not the kind of car you pick up a fifty-year-old millionaire in.

I started looking around for a car that said, "You have to be forty years old to drive me." At the same time, I didn't want something too fancy and I had to keep my budget in mind—which was vastly depleted after purchasing my new business suits. I found a brand-new Oldsmobile 98 Regency. Instant credibility. This car was huge. I think it slept twelve.

I even had gray put into my hair just around the temples. I know it was extreme, but I was desperate. In fact, I happened to be at a party attended by a good friend of the family's, a well-known plastic surgeon. I went up to him and asked, "Doc, how much would it cost for a face-drop?"

He informed me that the problem would solve itself in time and promptly recommended a good psychologist.

Now I was ready to work on my next fifty-year-old millionaire. A potential new client, and I left nothing to chance. I was to pick him up at his office so we could have lunch at his fancy country club to talk business. I pulled into the visitor's spot right near the front door of the two-story office complex. Before I turned the car off to go inside and get him, I tuned the radio to a beautiful music station, the kind of lush instrumental elevator music that says, "You have to be forty years old to listen to me."

After a forty-five-minute wait, we return to my huge car. We get in. On the seat between us is a small bottle of Geritol strategically resting atop the current issue of *Modern Maturity* magazine next to a box of suppositories. I put the key in the ignition. As the car comes to life, the power antenna rises and the car fills with a lush instrumental of Percy Faith playing "Stairway to Heaven." After just a few seconds I reach across to turn the radio off so we can begin our talk, but in just those few seconds, I know I made a very important impression on this gentleman.

Obviously impressed so far, he thoughtfully asked, "By the way, Jeff, how old are you?"

It became apparent then that I had to deal directly with that question of "How old are you?" And I had to do it without lying. You never lie to a client. It was a question I struggled with for many weeks before the answer hit me. When a client would ask me, "By the way, Jeff, how old are you?" I'd look him right straight in the eye and respond, "I'll be thirty-nine in April!" This is true. It happens to be in 1995. My mother liked it so much she uses it in reverse: "I was forty-nine in February" (we won't say which February).

Notice that when I looked around for a car, I didn't immediately buy a Cadillac or Mercedes. I only wanted to have a car that would give me enough of an appearance of success that I wouldn't get discounted before I had an opportunity to talk with the client. The Oldsmobile 98 Regency was fine for that purpose. If I started driving a

Mercedes 450 SL, I think it would have put the clients *en garde* again just as the Opel did. Balance is key.

Despite what anyone tells you, image is important. It's not the end-all because you have to back the image with results. Image won't necessarily get you a client, but it will help you at least get an honest hearing.

CHAPTER 3

Keeping Clients
Satisfied to Keep
Them Coming Back

While presenting a seminar in Hawaii, I had an accident and hurt my knee. I made it through the program. Then, when I returned home, I made an appointment with a knee specialist because it was still causing me discomfort and making it difficult to get around. After thirty minutes in the waiting room and another ten minutes waiting in the examining room, the doctor looked at my knee and looked at my X rays and determined that there was no damage. It was strained and would eventually heal itself. He scheduled an appointment for a month later just to see that everything was fine.

A month later my knee was fine. No more problem but I kept the appointment. After a forty-five-minute wait this time, I left. If I injure my knee again, I'll find another doctor.

Legal Lethal. Last year, after renting office space for the previous eleven years, we purchased an office building. Over the years we've worked with about three different law firms, specializing in different areas as the need came up. When we needed an attorney to work with on this building purchase, we called a couple of law firms that dealt mostly on our business affairs in the past. They weren't prompt in returning our phone calls and we needed some answers pronto!

We then called a third attorney, who was referred to us by someone we trusted. He tried to convince us we needed some unrelated services. I knew from past experience that this wasn't necessary. It seemed to me he was only interested in hitting us up for about five hundred dollars in fees for a service we didn't need.

The last firm we called worked with us on our pension program. We called for a recommendation and fortunately they had an attorney on staff who specialized in real estate law. She was wonderful. She returned all our phone calls promptly and did a magnificent job. We've used her for other real estate deals and referred her to friends and real estate agents.

Now we use this firm for more of our corporate work whenever possible. And as for that poor shlub who wanted to make a quick five hundred on us, it cost him tens of thousands of dollars in fees over the next few years. That's not to mention loss of referrals we give to people who do good work at reasonable fees for us. Big mistake.

Steve Trotter is a successful attorney and sole practitioner in Fort Wayne, Indiana. He is quick to point out that the most important element of developing a successful clientele is good service. His marketing, including his own call-in radio show, is important but does not replace the need to provide quality work at a fair price. He also stresses that one of the most important and often most difficult aspects is returning phone calls promptly. To try to get back to clients promptly, Steve has even started calling some of them in the evening from his home. Many clients appreciate that they are important enough to warrant this kind of service.

Client Revolution Solution

There is and has been a consumer revolution going on. The consumer is demanding higher quality and better service. And whether you call your client a patient, customer, patron, or sponsor, one thing is clear. To be successful in the future, you have to keep your existing clients very happy.

Obviously this is nothing new in organizations that have used marketing and advertising all along. But it is new in most professions and service industries. Jump on this trend now or you'll get trampled over. It means you're going to do things you've never dreamed of doing before. Little things, like returning phone calls promptly.

In his book *Managing the Future*, Robert Tucker lists customer service as one of the ten main driving forces of change in the nineties.[15] He notes four reasons for this:

1. Today's harried life-styles mean that people value service more than ever.
2. It's the surest way to differentiate your business from your competitor's.
3. It's the surest way to build and sustain a competitive advantage.
4. It's increasingly important, even for discounters.

Dr. Neil Baum is a urologist in private practice in New Orleans. Dr. Baum feels that most physicians trans-

---

[15]*Managing the Future: 10 Driving Forces of Change for the '90s,* by Robert B. Tucker (New York: G. P. Putnam's Sons, 1991).

late marketing into advertising and doctors are very uncomfortable with advertising. He feels that marketing is
going that extra mile, service above and beyond the call,
making your office user-friendly and making amenities for
patient care. Dr. Baum told us:

> "The best way to market a practice is to call the
> patient at home. A doctor that calls at home will do
> much public relations and public image building for
> the practice. The patients are in disbelief that a doctor
> would call them at home. It reassures them and allows
> the doctor to anticipate patient problems by talking
> with them."

He thinks about his practice from the patient's point
of view. For example, he uses reading material in his
reception area targeted for his patients. I can't remember
how often I've been forced to read a two-year-old copy of
People magazine.

Dr. Baum further cautions, "I want to emphasize that
marketing is not a substitute for good medicine. This
differentiates your practice from the rest."

A young cardiologist in Florida has an understanding
with his patients. Because he's a sole practitioner and on
call always, patients can end up waiting hours for their
appointments. This he can't help. Still, when they're sick,
he's there at a moment's notice. His patients appreciate
his honesty up front and his lifesaving service when it's
needed most.

One common thread that we constantly came across
when researching this book was that the most effective
forms of marketing included word of mouth and referrals.
One can hardly argue with this but unfortunately it's not
enough. Even so, to get the referrals and word of mouth,
you have to have satisfied clients.

What Is a Satisfied Client?

Good question. And there is a very simple answer. *It's what the client says is satisfaction.* It's not *your* definition that counts. You may provide the best service or have the best product, yet if the client is unhappy, it's for naught. You have to figure out what is important to your clients. And the best way to do that, simply, is to ask.

We buy our computers for our office from one company in town because they provide us good service. Their computers are reasonably priced while other places locally have the same or similar machines available for a little less. We buy only from this company because we know they'll take care of us. If we have a question, they answer it. If there's a problem with a machine, they fix it fast or replace it.

From time to time, as we expand our operation, we need more computers. We're tempted to buy them a little cheaper from some of the other places. But we invariably decide against it because we're not just paying for the "box" but for the support that comes with it.

We did have a problem with our computer supplier. Every time we called them we got put on hold with their voice-mail system for way too long. We'd wait as much as fifteen minutes to get through. As can be expected, we weren't their only customer with this problem. Since we really like this supplier, we let them know about this frustration we were having. As a result, they installed a new system to make it easier for customers to get through.

Had this been any other supplier, we would not have bothered to let them know. According to Dr. Michael LeBoeuf, author of the best-seller *How to Win Customers and Keep Them for Life*:

A typical business hears from only 4 percent of its dissatisfied customers. That means that the remaining 96 percent aren't going to give you a second chance. They're just going to smile, take their business elsewhere, and tell their friends about the lousy service you gave. On the other hand, a complaining customer is being honest with you and giving you another opportunity to make good.[16]

Sometimes there's not much you can do about certain elements that may be annoying to your clients. So you need to look at a creative approach to lessen the problem as much as possible. One of the more creative approaches to waiting on the phone for help is used by the WordPerfect organization in Orem, Utah. We used WordPerfect (version 5.1) for writing this book as well as other writing projects. I had a question about a function, so I called their toll-free number to see if they could offer a solution. As expected, the phone is answered by a computer voice-mail system that can, through my Touch-Tone phone, direct my call. I was given some options based on specific problem areas. Then I was again greeted by a computer telling me that all lines are busy but to please wait, I will be helped soon.

I expected to be put on hold for quite a while, and as expected I was treated to music on hold. It was followed by what sounded like a local radio station giving a typical traffic report—except this traffic report was of the telephone traffic waiting to get through to the support people:

---

[16]*How to Win Customers and Keep Them for Life,* by Dr. Michael LeBoeuf, Ph.D. (New York: G. P. Putnam's Sons). Also available as an audiocassette album through Nightingale-Conant, Chicago. Video available through Calley Curtis, Hollywood, Calif.

". . . and if waiting for help on installation, you have about three people ahead of you. So you can expect, oh, about a two-to-three-minute wait. And for those of you waiting for help with features, you have about six in front of you; it'll be just another five minutes so hang in there. By the way, if you have a Mac you'd be interested to know that we just came out with . . ."

This approach was so fascinating that I called Word-Perfect and interviewed Dave Webb, who is one of three "hold jockeys." They get their incoming phone traffic information on screen from the voice-mail system, tell listeners how long they have to wait or how many people are ahead of them, and promote new products and play music. Imagine how much "hold jockeys" could help an airline reduce your frustration when calling to see if your flight is on time.

It was after working with a few different software companies and their well-developed telephone support staff that we got an idea for some Streetfighting support. We market a package of material called the "Streetfighter's Profit Package" that has one videotape, two audio albums, and two books. The cost is $350. The problem with most off-the-shelf training programs is that you have no place to go if you have a question.

So, like the software companies, we added to the package, at no additional charge, telephone support. Any subscriber to our "Profit Package" can call our office and ask questions, brainstorm, or fine-tune ideas based on the information in the kit. If we're not in the office, we agree to return the call within twenty-four hours.

The response has been tremendous. We have doubled the number of "Profit Package" sales, but we found out an interesting side benefit we hadn't counted on. We're getting feedback on what's working and what's not out in the field. It's allowing us to become smarter and better about what we do because our own clients are educating us. Everybody wins.

Sure it's more work for us, but we make it up in volume of sales and we have no need to discount our products like other trainers do. We're adding value. We've even had clients buy the package solely for the telephone support rights. It's the cheapest consulting they can buy.

We organize this effort using TeleMagic software, so we have an instant record of our clients' past calls. We know their background plus the advice we gave in those calls. Sometimes we'll call them to see how things went. This creates some word of mouth.

Our next step, once we get too busy offering support, is to go to a special computerized voice-mail system. With every "Package" purchase we'll give the client his own mailbox number. If there's no one in the office to take the call, a client can leave his problem in the mailbox. Then, from the road, we can call in and offer our solution.

At his convenience the client can call his box for the answer. In addition, we plan to share some general marketing ideas. We will put it into all the mailboxes about once a week so they can get the hottest ideas or share the newest success stories...kind of an audio newsletter.

We estimate we'll be needing this technology very soon. We want all the bugs worked out before we really need it. Anticipating future trends and client expectations is another key to keeping your clients satisfied now and in the future.

Seven Easy Steps to Happier Clients

Here are a few ways in which you can help keep your clients a little happier:

1. If you make a promise, keep it. Jerry Wilson, author of *Word-of-Mouth Marketing*, interviewed Jack Miller, of Quill, a leading mail-order firm in office supplies:

> One of my managers told me that we missed an air shipment to Texas. It was promised, but he said that the order would have to wait until next day. I asked why we should wait. He said if we used any other way, it would cost us $250. That's more than the profit we were making on this order. Who the hell cares? We promised the customer. It's our fault, not his. We shipped it. If you can't do something, that's a different story. You tell the customer you can't. But you have to keep your promises.[17]

2. If for some reason you can't make good on your promise, let the client know as soon as possible. Be honest and straight with the client. Keep him informed of your progress and negotiate a new objective or deadline. If there is inconvenience or loss to your client because you can't do what you said you could, contemplate offering some consideration.

Let the client know that this in no way makes up for the broken promise but is a gesture to let the client know how much you value his business. This consideration can be a discount, additional services, free gift (like a dinner for two). Use your common sense. Don't make it too great or too little.

3. Answer phones promptly. No more than three rings. Answer with enthusiasm. Make sure that the receptionist is smiling and has a pleasant voice. A smile

---

[17]*Word-of-Mouth Marketing*, by Jerry R. Wilson (New York: John Wiley & Sons, 1991), p. 65.

comes through on the phone. You're not doing the client a favor by answering this call; he's doing you one. The client permits you to stay in business and make a living. Don't put someone on hold too long. If you can't get to him, offer to return the call.

4. Don't make people wait. Not in your office, in theirs, or at some other location. You set a time, be there on time. If you're going to run late, call as soon as you know you'll be late.

5. Communicate. Assume the client knows nothing. Make sure the client knows what the cost is and what he or she will get. Avoid hidden costs. Bring them out in the open. Give realistic ranges. Don't inflate possible results or underestimate risks. Clients appreciate honesty and decry even the slightest misdirection.

6. Encourage honest feedback. You hear many people asking, "How am I doing?" This does *not* encourage honest feedback. It's more likely to get a perfunctory "Okay." Instead, ask, "If I could change one thing about what we did for you, what would it be?" This question encourages clients to help you improve. Once you get an answer, don't defend yourself. Simply thank the client for the input. Then ask the question again. "If we could have changed one other thing, what would it be?" If appropriate, follow up their answer with "Why?" This gets you more detail.

Once you've gotten all the feedback from a client, look for ways of dealing with the comments. Whether or not the comment was "fair" or legitimate, it was the client's perception.

Telephone and mail surveys are fine, but spend some time one-to-one with clients for getting feedback as well.

7. Sell only what the client wants or needs. This doesn't mean you shouldn't try to market additional products or services. You should. However, if a certain

product or service is of no value to the client, don't take advantage.

One very hot summer, my in-laws' air conditioner went out. They were convinced that it needed to be replaced and had called Mr. Hanzel to replace it. He repaired all their major appliances in the past. He's prompt, reasonable, and a nice person to deal with. The next day he comes out with a brand-new central air-conditioning unit on his truck ready for installation. After a few minutes of surveying the situation he reported back to my father-in-law that he really didn't need a new air conditioner. There was only a minor problem with the old one.

Mr. Hanzel fixed the old one and charged his standard service fee. He could easily have sold my in-laws the new unit for many thousands of dollars. How many people do you think have heard that story? How many people want Mr. Hanzel doing all their repair and replacement work?

Following these seven commonsense steps will help you gain more word-of-mouth referrals. It also ensures that when you do some basic marketing to get new clients, you'll keep them. Marketing can only help you get potential clients to make a call or visit you. It's up to you to develop a good long-term relationship.

CHAPTER 4

Dominating Your Market With Public Speaking

Public speaking gets you in front of potential clients. It gives you credibility, exposure, and it usually costs you nothing. Developing and promoting your public speaking is a subtle yet exceedingly effective marketing tool.

Your presentations can follow three basic formats: speeches, seminars, and workshops. These three formats are very much related and there is often a fine distinction from one to the other.

The Speech. The speech uses the least amount of audience participation and is more of a one-way form of communication. You'll find this more appropriate when you're asked to speak to groups with limited time like at a business luncheon or after dinner. A speech can be the most difficult because you must present your ideas very clearly yet concisely. An effective speech often has the most entertaining of the three formats.

The Seminar. A seminar allows you to share information with your audience that, in turn, gives the audience an opportunity to discover something valuable about you. Many different types of businesses and professions use the seminar approach to getting clients. Seminars are inexpensive, bring many potential clients together at once, and give you authority. Seminars also require that you have a higher level of knowledge about your subject than does a speech.

The Workshop. A workshop has the most audience involvement. Besides giving information, a workshop leader often uses role-playing and exercises. This form of public speaking is more "hands-on." A workshop also seems to last much longer than a seminar or speech.

How Some Have Used Speaking to Get Results

Doctors. When a young doctor was just starting his pediatrics practice after finishing his residency in Phoenix, he used free seminars to help his practice through its infancy. His hospital sponsored prenatal-care seminars for expectant mothers, and he taught those seminars, free. It was a great public service for both the hospital and the pediatrician, and both received patients because of the effort.

A young cardiologist in central Florida used the same technique to build his practice. The only difference was that since senior citizens are his target group, it was very easy to find them already assembled. So he would go to their meeting places to conduct his seminars. It didn't take more than six months before he was swamped with patients.

Dr. Bruce Fraser, an oral surgeon in our office complex, gets most of his patients on referral from general dentists. When he has time, he takes the dentists out to lunch. He conducts seminars on implants at the local Ramada, at which he also brings in other technical experts to speak. He also likes to have groups of five dentists meet at his office where they can have a smaller, more personal workshop on new developments.

Lawyers. Frank Foster, an attorney specializing in copyrights, trademarks, and patents, wrote a book on the subject.[18] Because of his exposure from the book, he was asked to speak at the Ohio Chapter of the National Speakers Association. This is a group of about one hundred professional speakers who also write and produce original material. One of their biggest concerns is how to protect that information. Mr. Foster's seminar at this group's meetings was an excellent way to attract many potential clients who may need legal work in this area.

Insurance. A successful life insurance agent in Ohio has conducted many seminars over the years. It's not a new approach in this industry and he's the first to give the credit to others. Still, this agent has added some unique twists that allow him to infiltrate the millionaire level of potential clients.

Selling clients on attending a life insurance seminar is far different from selling clients on one presented by a doctor or lawyer. So he modified his approach. First, he contacted a dozen of his best clients with whom he had a very strong relationship. He merely told them that he was conducting a seminar on a new program. The seminar itself would last no more than twenty minutes and would be preceded by dinner.

The dinner was taking place at an exclusive club. Everything was first-class. To add more importance to this program, he brought in a featured speaker, an attorney in the insurance industry who was an expert on

---

[18]*Copyrights, Trade Marks, and Patents*, by Frank Foster and Robert L. Shook (New York: John Wiley & Sons, 1989).

tax law. The outside speaker certainly added an air of validity to the presentation.

Obviously this program cost him some bucks. But after the program he got his clients' feedback to it. Besides finding out the level of interest for this new product, he also asked each of those clients for ten people that they felt would benefit from seeing the presentation. In this way he used the seminar and dinner as a means to get referrals from outside his existing prime client base for future seminars. His goal was to build this program with "mirrors."

His associate worked out his version of the program on a smaller scale for a special product they developed to help parents save money for their children's college education. He conducted his program at day-care centers as an added value. The day-care center would provide the mailing list as well as mention the program in their regular mailings and internal displays.

He would use the client list for phone calls to see if there was interest. Those clients who were interested received a formal invitation to his program.

The parents who attended were obviously in need of some sort of saving and investment program to ensure that they could afford to send their children to college. He had the answer and presented that, as well as other competitive options, in his seminar. Then at the end the parents filled out a simple questionnaire that he used for follow-up later.

He really had to force himself to make cold calls by telephone, an activity vital to selling his product. Still, by working with day-care centers, calling a list that had been partially qualified, and calling specifically about a free seminar made the process much easier. Very little rejection.

Investments. Several years ago I had the opportunity of working with Minneapolis-based investment company

IDS. I was brought in to work specifically on the IRA program. One technique their agents used successfully was to hold investment seminars. They would usually run some advertising in the local newspaper and rent a meeting room at a local hotel. Their seminar gave the audience much information about how an individual retirement program worked and what they needed to do to start one.

I suggested a slight variation that had been tested by one of their more successful agents. Instead of paying for the newspaper advertising and renting a room, I suggested that they approach organizations or churches about the same program. Turn it into a fund-raiser.

The agent would approach, for example, a church where he felt most of the parishioners were in the market for an IRA. He would offer to provide a seminar at their location. For every "qualified" congregant that attended the seminar, he would donate five dollars. If they reached certain other attendance goals, like twenty-five, fifty, and so on, there would be additional donations. It was up to the Ladies' Auxiliary, or whatever internal group at the church, to contact their congregants and get them to attend. They could call, mail (at the nonprofit rate), make announcements, and put up bulletins.

The advantage of this approach is that there is no risk. With traditional advertising or direct mail you pay whether you get attendees or not. But in the fund-raising approach, you get the same benefit with no risk. You only pay for the qualified people that show. Not only that but you're a hero, since you end up, hopefully, writing a big check to the congregation. Everybody wins.

Wigs. I met a speaker at one of the National Speakers Association conventions who conducted seminars on wigs for women receiving chemotherapy. She gave her seminar free, sponsored by a hospital. She found that she would usually sell about ten of these very high-quality wigs as a result. That would translate to about $10,000 worth of sales for a one-hour seminar. She had no marketing costs and her only direct expenses were for the wigs. The rest was profit.

Counseling. Duffy Spencer, Ph.D., is a social psychologist in Long Island. To help build her practice, she approached Nassau Community College about teaching a course for their adult education program. Five hundred thousand catalogs are mailed each term to promote the courses she offers. The college pays very little for teaching the courses, but the exposure of half a million advertising pieces is worth it. And the credibility she gains through her association with the college further helps her promote her private practice.

Professional Speaker. I make my living by giving speeches and seminars. I get a fee for them and can't afford to do them free. Yet there came an opportunity that I couldn't pass up. The American Booksellers Association was having their annual trade show. This is a massive event and every publisher participates. I had an opportunity to be a presenter at this show. The audience would be primarily bookstore owners and managers. When you're also selling books for a living, it's invaluable to have an opportunity to present your program for hundreds of people who can make your book successful.

The problem was that they don't pay their speakers. Not only that, you have to pay your own expenses! Well, to every rule there is an exception and I made one here. The opportunity to advance my career was great, so I agreed. I was even able to get one of my publishers to pay my expenses.

Because of this free speech, my publishers started giving me more preferential treatment. Keep in mind that they have hundreds of authors, so anything you can do to get them to take special notice of you is very important. I also got some great exposure in *Publishers Weekly*. And, of course, hundreds of booksellers heard and met me. When my books come in, I think they'll be a little more inclined to recommend it and display perhaps a little more than some others. After all, they have hundreds of business book titles with which to work.

How to Discover Your Opportunities From the Platform

We have just seen a few examples of how people promote their business or career with public speaking. You now need to look at your situation and apply some basic ideas to see how you can take advantage of these opportunities.

Target Audience. You first need to identify your ideal target audience as described earlier. With what type of clients do you do business now? What type of clients would you prefer to do business with in the future? What do these people or businesses have in common?

People Magnet. Once you've determined the type of target audience you want, and what they have in common, you need to go to the next step. You want an audience that is made up of a significant number of potential clients. So look for the best "people magnets." A people magnet is any organization or business that attracts a specific type of people.

If you're looking to reach small business owners, you probably would *not* want to address your local Boy Scout group. You must determine where they gather en masse. Small business people might attend functions for the Chamber of Commerce or an entrepreneurial association. They often attend business-related trade shows or expos. And they might be reachable with the cooperation of any local successful business that serves other businesses like office supply, computers, office furniture, or copy machines.

A good example of finding the right people magnet was used by Jeff Herman, the literary agent from New York mentioned earlier. Jeff is always looking for talented writers and authors. He found an organization that was filled with members who are authors or want to be authors. It's the National Speakers Association. Jeff was first brought to the Ohio Speakers Forum, the Ohio chapter of NSA. The seminar he gave was so successful that he joined the national organization and was asked to present at a convention. Between his seminars and meeting people at the conventions, he has picked up many clients from this group. At the same time, his unique expertise is valuable to members of this organization. Everyone benefits from the relationship.

Sponsorship. Getting a sponsor for your presentation cuts down your risk. With a sponsor you have less investment in time or money. Without a sponsor you may have to consider other advertising options like newspaper, direct mail, radio, TV, telemarketing, to attract people to your seminar.

Outline. Next you need to figure out what you want to say. It's important to give your audience valuable, practical information without giving away the store at the same time. You also must not be a constant commercial. Depending on the amount of time you have, you need to figure out what you want to accomplish in this presentation. What are the main points you wish to make?

When giving a speech, it's best to keep the main points to a minimum. You don't want to give so much information that your listeners are overwhelmed. Try making two or three main points, then embellish those points with success stories, anecdotes, quotes, and even humor to drive home those points. At the same time you don't want to come off arrogant. Success stories are important, but share the success with the client in the story. Make your clients the heroes, not you. People will only remember a small amount of the information you give them. This is why it is important to give them few ideas but really make those ideas stick.

Continue working on your outline. A speech should have a beginning, middle, and end. Ideally you don't want to *read* your speech. You should have enough expertise about your subject that you can talk about it to your audience with only an outline. Use it to keep you on track and remind you of the main points.

Humor. Humor can be an important part of effective public speaking. According to Melvin Helitzer, author of *Comedy Writing Secrets,* "Humor is a universal speech opener because it immediately gets us respectful attention. It's psychologically impossible to hate someone with whom you've laughed."[19] And if you want an audience to remember your key points, illustrate those points with humor.

Just telling jokes to get a laugh doesn't necessarily make impact with your audience. You're not there to do a stand-up routine. And your humor doesn't have to be a laugh a minute. The most effective humor is original humor. Humor is often a funny story based on a personal experience that helps your audience remember a key point. Humor is all around you, so look for it. Don't try to be a comedian but do look for real-life examples to illustrate your key points. (These examples do not necessarily have to be humorous. You can also use some very dramatic stories as well.)

---

[19]*Comedy Writing Secrets: How to Think Funny, Write Funny, Act Funny, and Get Paid for It,* by Melvin Helitzer (Cincinnati: Writer's Digest Books, 1987).

A warning about humor. Avoid profanity and ethnic jokes. You might be able to get away with it with certain audiences, but invariably the most innocent comment offends someone. Be careful. Remember, the purpose of your public speaking is to build credibility and get more clients. That is more difficult if members of your audience are upset with some derogatory comment you've made.

Practice. Find a no-liability group to whom you can practice. This practice group ideally should have no one in the audience that you would normally go after as a client. You want a group there so you can work out the bugs in your presentation. Don't expect to give a polished presentation immediately. That's okay. That's part of the process. But you don't want to practice on an audience comprised of fifty of your biggest potential clients.

There are many organizations that constantly look for luncheon speakers like Kiwanis, Optimists, Elk, Rotary, Lions. If their members are *not* your typical clientele, offer to do programs for them. It's great practice.

Have your sessions recorded. Listening to yourself on audio or watching yourself on video shot with your camcorder helps you see yourself the way the audience does. It may feel strange to watch or listen to yourself, but there is no better way for you to improve your platform skills. From those tapes take one area that you want to improve. Perhaps you are using some gesture too much or using too many "ahhs" or "umms" throughout. Once you've heard or seen it, it's much easier to correct.

For improving your presentation skills, consider joining your local chapter of Toastmasters. It's also a wonderful way to develop your speaking style and get some practice working in front of a group.

To help get over typical stage fright, you might consider trying out for a small part in a community play. The production is totally removed from your normal line of work, so it is less threatening. What it will do is give you an opportunity to work onstage in front of an audience. Public speaking is the biggest fear, even more so than death, to most people. Do things that help you get out more so that you become more and more comfortable from the platform. According to Bill Brooks, an accomplished public speaker and author of *High Impact Public Speaking:*

> All you need is a few great successes at speaking and you will find yourself hopelessly hooked for life. There's something about standing before an audience and having them respond warmly to you that creates an overpowering desire to keep doing it, and to do it better and better.[20]

Watch professional speakers as much as you can, not to copy their material but to see their style. Watch how they emphasize their points. Observe how they use their body, voice, pauses, eye contact with the audience, and even their "ad-libs" (most of which are probably rehearsed well in advance). The more you observe, the better an idea you'll have of your own capabilities and talents.

Lastly you may want to consider, when you're ready, using a vocal or acting coach to help you improve your presentation style. A good coach can see what you're doing and help you with your diction, body movement, volume, pitch, and timing. These same techniques, by the way, are very useful when making presentations in the boardroom or a client's conference room as well.

---

[20]*High Impact Public Speaking,* by William T. Brooks (Englewood Cliffs, N.J.: Prentice-Hall, 1988).

Where to Find Examples for Guidance

You may want to visit your local or state chapter of the National Speakers Association.[21] Since you probably do not want to become a professional speaker, at least not yet, this is *not* an organization I'd recommend you join (you're much better off with Toastmasters), but you can usually attend a few meetings as a guest just to observe how the presenters perform.

Most NSA chapters sponsor a "showcase." This is a special event where about twenty speakers each get ten to fifteen minutes to present in front of an audience filled primarily with meeting planners (a very good target audience for professional speakers). If you have an opportunity, you may wish to go. It will give you great exposure to many different types of speakers...and lunch is often included in the price of admission!

There is another special program that some local NSA chapters sponsor called "Speakers School." This is one event geared more for the amateur speaker and borderline professional speaker. A variety of topics are covered, much of them dealing with developing materials, platform skills, marketing, and other aspects of the business of speaking. It's also a great opportunity to observe some of the better speakers on the local, state, and even national level.

Another way to observe professional speakers is to see their demo videos. To do this, consider getting involved in an association or within your company for the hiring of a professional speaker. Perhaps your local Chamber of

---

[21]National Speakers Association, 3877 N. 7th St., Ste. 350, Phoenix, AZ 85014. (602) 265-1001.

Commerce or trade association is going to need a professional speaker for a dinner, convention, or special event. To help you with the selection, contact a credible speakers' bureau. A speakers' bureau works with "meeting planners" to find speakers.

Speakers' bureaus get paid a commission from the speaker for the booking, so it should cost you the same. However, by working with a bureau you'll have access to hundreds of speakers. The bureau will narrow it down as much as you want. When they have an idea of what kind of speaker you want and the fee range you'll pay, they start sending you video demo tapes. These tapes are usually live recordings of segments of presentations and may contain some "promotional" material as well. For a list of NSA member bureaus and agents you can contact the National Speakers Association and they'll send it to you free. (If you would like a copy of our ten-minute demo video, send $20 plus $3 shipping to Demo Video, Streetfighter Marketing, 467 Waterbury Ct., Gahanna, OH 43206.)

Handouts. To leverage your presentation, prepare a leave-behind piece that audience members can take home with them after your presentation. It can be a simple outline, bullet points, or fill in the blanks. It does not have to be a great deal of copy, just a reminder of the main points you were trying to make. Be sure that your name, business, address, and phone appear at the top or bottom of every sheet in your handout. Make it easy for people to get in touch with you later if they want to. Notice that we suggest it appear on every sheet. The reason is that some sheets may get separated. Even if you have a ten- or twenty-page handout, use a header or footer with all the information.

It is appropriate to use your company logo, the company name, address, and phone number on the cover sheet, but these items should not dominate the cover. The title of the presentation and perhaps the organization name or logo should dominate. Keep your "plug" visible but subtle. For the remainder of the sheets, again put it at the bottom. This can be achieved subtly by using a copyright notice as a footer, which includes your name, company name, address, and phone.

Spend the time and money needed to create a professional-looking handout. You are using this presentation as a means to build credibility and get new clients. You want them to feel comfortable with you. You don't have to spend a fortune, though. Here's a few tricks.

First, if possible, create your sheets on a laser printer. It will look typeset and it's easy to do. Print the inside pages of your handout in plain white copy paper (20-pound). It's the cheapest, but consider having the front page printed on an attractive cover stock, perhaps in multiple colors if the budget permits. Just by changing the cover stock you add a great deal of professionalism to the piece without great expense. Use the same cover stock for your back cover. It doesn't have to be printed.

Ideas on Visual Aids

Think about what best enhances your presentation. Much of this depends on the type of presentation you will be giving. If there is some technical information, your first step is to do away with as much of it as you think you can. However, if you can't, then, in addition to your handout, you may wish to work with slides, overheads, or flip charts.

Slides and overheads can be prepared ahead of time and placed in order for your presentation. The highest quality will usually come from slides, but there is often some expense in setting them up. Keep your slides simple and only present the main points on-screen. Don't use a lot of copy, because the audience will have a difficult time reading it and will pay less attention to what you're saying.

For example, if I were presenting workshops on this chapter of the book, the slide that would be up right now would be "Visual Aids." That's it. It might have yellow type on a blue background. When I talk about slides, I probably would just have a title slide that said "Slides" and I might include some clip art of a picture of a slide. Very simple.

You can have an artist prepare title slides for you, or you can use computer programs like Harvard Graphics®[22] to create your title slides, graphs, pie charts, clip art, etc., that can then be transferred to slides. Just prior to each presentation, run through your slides to make sure they're in the right order and facing forward.

Overheads work the same way but are better for a smaller group. They also work better if you need more light in the room than with a slide projector. Overheads can be made on most photocopy machines or laser printers, so you can reproduce your handout on clear acetate for your presentation.

With overheads you do have a little more flexibility with your presentation. You can change the order at the last minute or address issues that you find are more important to that audience. This is more difficult with a slide show because you have to follow the order, then fast forward or backward to find the correct slides. But the advantage of slides is that they can serve as an outline or prompt in keeping you on track.

---

[22]Harvard Graphics is the registered trademark of Publishing Software Corporation, 1901 Landings Dr., P.O. Box 7210, Mountain View, CA 94039.

One last point about slides and overheads. Don't talk to the screen. If you must glance at the screen, that's fine, and you can even point at certain things, but do it briefly and then address your audience.

Flip charts are fine when you are doing audience participation to smaller groups. If you are making a point and want it written on the flip chart, have a volunteer from the audience do it. This allows you to focus your attention on the audience.

Practice writing fast and clearly. It sounds basic but it's important. You may wish to bring your own markers, since most meeting rooms provide ones that are usually anemic. The wider the better.

Props are another consideration, especially if you're selling and demonstrating a product. You have to make sure you've set up your room so the entire audience can see what you're doing. Getting audience involvement with the product is also a good way to get their participation and understanding of the value.

Making the Room Speaker-Friendly

If you have any control of the room setup, there are some elements that might help you get a better result. Keep the room just a little on the cool side, 68 to 70 degrees. Once the room fills up with people, it will get warm, and it's much more difficult working with people in a warm room. This is particularly important if your presentation is after a meal.

If there is to be writing, set your room up classroom style with tables. If not, you would be better off theater style. With either approach consider having it set up "chevron" style. This arrangement makes it easier for the

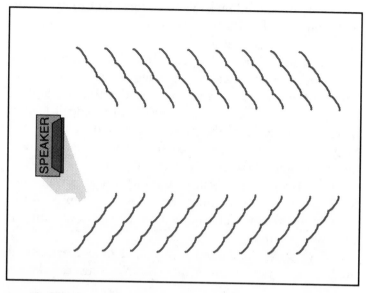

Figure 1. Chevron style puts the outside rows in a direct line of sight to the speaker.

people in the outer rows to participate. Chevron style has the chairs (and tables) set up in a "V."

When you don't know how many people will show up at your presentation, you might end up with half the seats empty. Most will likely sit in back. To avoid this problem, set up fewer rows but have extra chairs available, stacked in the back of the room. You can then add chairs in the back, as needed.

Some may argue that this gives the impression that you're not organized enough to anticipate the crowd. However, I feel it gives the impression that the turnout was so overwhelmingly successful that you had to set up more chairs at the last minute. This last-minute craziness to get the chairs up actually adds to the energy of the room. No problem in starting five or even ten minutes late. But you should make an announcement to the group that you will be starting in five minutes so that the latecomers can get settled.

Most rooms are rectangular. Tom Winninger, a highly respected professional speaker, suggests you set up on the long wall, not the short wall, like most people do. Setting up on the short wall makes it much more difficult for the people in the back of the room to see. Setting up on the long wall means the distance from you to the furthest person is much less. Set the lectern (and risers if they're used) on the opposite wall or the furthest long wall from the entrance to the room. Keep water and display in the back except those items you will be demonstrating during your presentation.

If you are using a microphone, double-check sound quality and the room acoustics. Nothing can kill a

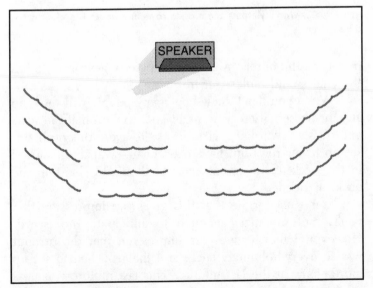

Figure 2. Setting the lectern on the long wall brings the furthest members of the audience closer to the speaker.

presentation faster than feedback or a mike that makes funny noises. When using a wireless microphone, have a wired mike on standby just in case you start getting air traffic control instructions from the airport through the sound system. For wired mikes, have enough cord on the microphone to move around if that's your style.

Leave nothing to chance. If there are phones in the room, have them disconnected. If there are servers taking plates, make sure they know not to do so when you start. Talk to the meeting planner and the person in charge of the room days in advance and go over your room requirements. Make sure they understand. Draw diagrams if need be. Go to the meeting at least an hour ahead of time to deal with last-minute problems that invariably come up.

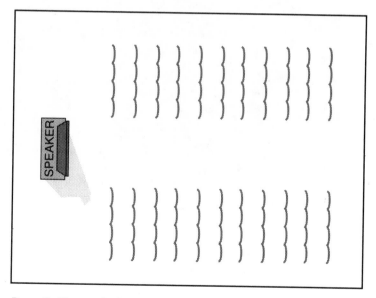

Figure 3. The standard room setup keeps the back half of the audience too far away.

Don't worry about butterflies. It happens to everyone, even the professionals. Marc and I do well over one hundred presentations a year and get nervous before each one. Channel that nervousness. Take deep slow breaths in through your nose and out through your mouth. I learned this in Lamaze class. It didn't help much for my wife's c-section, but it works great before *my* delivery.

Public speaking is a powerful marketing tool for you. The key is to practice and to perform.

How to Use Publicity to Get Clients to Come to You

Publicity enhances your credibility while providing you an effective yet subtle way to get clients. Publicity encompasses a wide range of marketing techniques. Most of these techniques get you media exposure. The three key differences between publicity exposure and advertising media exposure are:

1. Publicity can make more impact than advertising.
2. Publicity generally is more credible than advertising.
3. Publicity is free.

You can't exchange one for the other because they serve two different marketing needs. If it is appropriate for you to use advertising, publicity can enhance it. If you're uncomfortable with advertising, publicity provides you an acceptable alternative.

Advertising vs. Publicity

Advertising suffers from overexposure. Advertising people call it "clutter." There is so much advertising that people have a tendency to tune out most of it. There have been many estimates on the amount of advertising that you are exposed to daily. They range from five hundred to seventeen hundred commercial messages every day. From the minute you wake up in the morning and put on your Fruit of the Looms® underwear or cross your heart with Platex®, till you brush your teeth at night with Crest® Tartar Control, jump in your Serta Perfect Sleeper®, and set your GE® alarm clock, you're constantly bombarded with advertising.

You can't get away from it. Advertising is everywhere: radio, TV, newspapers, magazines, billboards, buses, benches, and blimps. There's no escape. Since there is so much advertising, people ignore most of it. Our brains protect us. There is no way we could remember all those messages and still be sane. So the brain blocks out most of them. Our brains have a buffer that filters through only a few of those messages every day. As a result, the vast majority of the billions and billions of dollars spent on advertising is wasted.

On the other hand, publicity allows you to burst through that brain buffer. When you're interviewed on a radio talk show or quoted in your local newspaper, you are not advertising. You are part of the news or entertainment, which is the main reason people use the media— entertainment. According to Steve Simon, of S&S Public Relations in Northbrook, Illinois:

> "I think publicity is worth at least ten times the value
> of the same space or airtime as traditional advertising.
> People know you can't buy your way onto the front

page of the *Chicago Tribune* or on *Oprah*. The audience pays attention during your interview but goes to the bathroom during the commercials!"

Unlike advertising, publicity is free. That is, there is no cost for the airtime or space. The downside of publicity is that, unlike advertising, you can't automatically get it whenever you want to. Moreover, you have little control, if any, of the content of your story. To be successful at publicity, you have to understand what the editors and reporters want. And I'll give you a hint: They're not interested in giving you free advertising.

Publicity may be your only choice for media exposure if your profession frowns on advertising. For many professionals there was a time advertising wasn't allowed. Those restrictions, for most, have been eased quite a bit. Yet it's still considered, by some, undignified.

At one time the only way a professional could advertise was to run for public office. A doctor could run for the office of coroner, a lawyer for prosecutor, an accountant for auditor. They could buy regular advertising and say what a success they were in their profession. This was good for some name recognition. The only problem with that approach is that they might win the election and then they'd really be in trouble.

Working With a Public Relations Firm

With all the advantages of publicity, you still have to convince a reporter or editor to do the story. This is the hard part. One way is to hire a public relations firm or publicist. Good ones are worth their weight in gold. At the same time you have to be careful. It's possible to spend a lot of money and have very little to show for it.

In our early years we used publicity as a primary medium to promote our Streetfighter Marketing company. While working with Steve Simon, of S&S Public Relations, we received a feature story in *Inc. Magazine*'s "Marketing & Selling" feature. The impact was wonderful. We had many people calling and writing to inquire about our services. The problem was that we weren't really prepared for the response. Besides consulting and seminars, we were promoting our book. But we lacked promotional material to sell these products and services. Even so, by sending out dustcovers and some makeshift promo information we managed to sell quite a few and pick up some clients. When the inquiries stopped, we had the article itself to use in our info kit.

We should have been better prepared. Once you get media coverage, it's a waste not to have the marketing systems in place to take advantage of the opportunity. Well, about eighteen months later we had such an opportunity. Steve came through again...only this time with *The Wall Street Journal*! Before this, however, we were slowly improving our ability to take advantage of leads generated from publicity and other sources.

It was important for us to create some "off-the-shelf products" that we could sell to small businesses who couldn't afford our consulting services. So we recorded one of our seminars and turned it into an audiocassette album with a ninety-page workbook. We also took all the articles we wrote and packaged them into an attractive three-ring binder with a table of contents. The audio album, collected articles, and book allowed us to offer a package worth a couple of hundred dollars.

Another important step for us was that we arranged to accept Visa, MasterCard, and American Express orders. This was very important for people who would call about our products. If we just sent them information, the likelihood of a sale was less than 50 percent. If they could order right then with a credit card, we would sell 95 percent of the interested callers.

The Wall Street Journal article was released on Wednesday, October 23, 1983. It was better than we ever dreamed. It appeared on the front page of the second section with a picture! The impact was phenomenal. The calls started at 6:00 A.M. and didn't end till 10:00 that night. The next three weeks were solid phone calls. The calls continued with regularity for the next three months. And even for the next two to three years there seemed to be at least one phone call a week from this article.

We obviously sold many of our packages and got many clients, and of course we use that article to this day in our information kit. Eventually we'll take out the picture, but the article is good forever. You probably don't sell tapes and books by phone. But the point here is that you must be prepared to take advantage of opportunities when they come up. This may mean setting up an appointment or getting a name, address, and phone for follow-up. It's the PR firm's job to get you the interview. Your challenge is to convert that exposure into paying clients.

HOW PR FIRMS WORK

Most PR firms work on a retainer fee. For a monthly fee, plus expenses, they'll develop your press kit, press release, cover letter, find the appropriate list of media contacts, and then do the contacting. They'll sell the reporters on you or your unique concept.

There are a few who will work on contingency. You pay them nothing, or a small fee for creating your press kit. When they get you the interview, then you pay them. You have much less risk this way. They often work from a menu of fees. They'll list all the major shows or publications and charge you a flat rate if you get published. They might also charge a flat rate per city if you're doing a tour, say, to promote a book. This can work great if you have a client in a different city. While you're there, they can set up interviews with the local newspaper, a TV news show, and perhaps a radio talk show. People who work on contingency are in the minority. They're usually people who are just getting started on their own.

Also find out the different circumstances where you pay. There's a big difference between getting interviewed and having the article appear. There's also a big difference between a mention and a full feature.

It's important, when considering a PR firm, to understand how they work and what are realistic expectations. If you're going to go this route, be fair. Give them enough time to do the job. A minimum of six months is fair. Anything less is tying their hands. You should start to see some decent interviews in the first three months. Hopefully you get enough exposure to at least break even. This may be somewhat of a judgment call on your part. Don't expect to make *Larry King Live* or the cover of *Time* right off the bat, if at all. By the same token, you'll never get the big stories if you don't stick it out.

Work with them to let them know what you want and what you don't want. Sometimes it's easy to get local radio interviews, yet you may find that they don't bring you the clients you want. There's nothing wrong with doing the radio show, but you don't want the account executive who is working with you to feel too secure about your business. Just because they're getting you these radio shows, for example, they equate activity with success. Not necessarily so. Explain to them what you think you need to make this work. Now, everyone can't get in *The Wall*

Street Journal, but you can create a list, with their help, of publications that can help you get clients.

If you have to narrow it down, you might be better off in print. Print exposure is easier to adapt into your marketing information kit. Even if you get no clients from an article, it is still impressive and builds credibility. We once got a small feature in the Money section of *USA Today.* It was on the second page with a photo. We didn't get one phone call. This is such a well-known publication we were surprised, but you just never know with publicity. Regardless, we still place the article in our information kit with the blue *USA Today* masthead at the top and it is impressive. You do a bad radio show and you have nothing to show for it.

Eric Yaverbaum, of Jericho Productions in New York, is an aggressive public relations person. When first starting out on his own, he had more time than money. So he used his expertise in public relations to help get his new PR firm off the ground. To draw attention to his new company, he needed to find a cause that he felt strongly about and could champion. He also needed a vehicle to gain the exposure he needed to attract the attention of potential clients.

His opportunity came with the 1984 baseball strike. Eric and his partner, John Sawyer, organized the "Fan's Strike." Because of this event they appeared on *Good Morning America* seven times, *Nightline, CBS This Morning,* the *Today* show twice, and in *USA Today* six times (twice in the Money section), *Newsweek,* and *Business-Week.* At that time they had just one client. As a result of their own publicity effort they picked up nine more clients. It got their business up and running.

Not only did they increase their account load tenfold but they made some very important media contacts in the process. That helped them provide their clients the same service they did for themselves.

The Ups and Downs of Doing Your Own Publicity

It is not necessary to use a PR firm to do your publicity. It can be done on your own. All you need is a little time, effort, and some basics.

PUBLICITY LEVELS

There are different levels to publicity. You can have anything from a major feature story all about you and your company to a little "blurb" or mention as part of another article. All types of positive publicity can be valuable. It is the combination of all the publicity you get, over time, that really helps you gain a level of awareness and credibility in your local market.

Network affiliates and some independents have newsrooms. They often produce news shows three times a day plus weekends (noon, six, and eleven). Each of those news shows is an opportunity for blurbs or features. Besides newscasts, there are talk shows and information shows. Radio talk shows provide many opportunities. Music-format radio usually has local news and special news shows. Phil Sorentino, a humor consultant, is a master at getting local publicity in Columbus, Ohio. He's gotten newspaper articles, TV and radio interviews. He finally got his own weekly five-minute radio slot on a major Columbus station. His focus has been the Columbus market. I know his show is making impact because one week he happened to mention my name and I got comments about it for several weeks after.

Most cities have a major daily, several tabloids, and

some specialty publications that may include a business publication, city magazine, and others.

Figure out the publications and specific news or talk shows where your clients are likely to be part of the audience. Once you know the media and specific features in which you would like to appear, you need an effective approach.

SELLING YOUR STORY TO THE MEDIA

The first step in selling your story to media is to have a story to sell. It has to be newsworthy. The media are not interested in giving you free advertising. They are concerned in providing interesting and valuable information to their audience.

Many others want this exposure as well. So, to grab their attention, you need a hook. The hook is the unique aspect or approach that causes a reporter to feel that the readers, listeners, or viewers want to know more about your subject.

To figure out what the media consider newsworthy, pay attention to their current stories. Read your local paper. Each section has a different editor: sports, business, religion, general news, government, food, entertainment, etc. Look at the types of stories they're using. Though they usually don't want to repeat a specific topic, you can find the "angle" to tie into that editor.

The Parker Shelton School of Karate in Fort Wayne received a great deal of publicity one year. One of their students had a public relations background, so he taught the owner how to get more publicity. The objective was to attract new students. First, they had many of their advanced members participating in tournaments regularly, similar to what you might have seen in the movie *The Karate Kid*. When students won, the results were called in to the sports editor of the local newspapers, the three network affiliates sportscasters, and a few of the radio station jocks. Usually there would be a mention in the newspaper plus a couple of shots on TV and radio.

Next they approached the Accent editor with self-defense ideas for women. This happened just after the paper had printed the latest FBI statistics on crime. Rapes and muggings were up. The school got a major feature story complete with a series of photos of students demonstrating various techniques. The "angle" was their enrollment increase at the school as it related to the FBI report. A noontime TV talk show picked up on it and the same was done live on TV.

Next they approached the business editor of the same newspaper and mentioned that the school had a number of business executives using karate as a means to help deal with stress. An unrelated article appeared later that year about different ways to develop a healthy heart, and some karate techniques taught at this school were mentioned.

By changing the angle to appeal to different editors and their audiences, this karate school got a variety of print and broadcast items which helped get new students. Some items pulled better than others, yet publicity was an integral part of their marketing program.

What is your unique angle that allows you to get press coverage? Regardless of the service or product you sell, there are always ways of presenting that information to get media coverage.

Attorney Steve Trotter is a sole practitioner who approached a local talk radio station about having a one-hour call-in show entitled *You and the Law*. Every week there would be a guest lawyer or two from the community answering questions about specific subjects. Callers would be invited to ask questions right on the air.

He's not paid to do this nor does it cost him anything,

but the exposure has been very rewarding, according to Steve. The show is on a small station on Sundays, and despite this nonprimetime exposure, he's very pleased with what is happening. Since the show began, he's busier than ever with new clients. He can't say that it's all due directly to the show but he feels it's a big contributor.

First, since he invites area lawyers on the show with him, he is developing very good relationships with many attorneys in town. He also invites nonattorney experts on subjects like tax law and medical malpractice. Though not his intent, this helped his networking and referral process greatly.

Many of his own clients tell him how much they like the show, so it is a great reinforcement. He also gets several phone calls at his office weekly as a result of the program. Listeners call to tell Steve that they heard him on the radio and have a question for him. As busy as he is, he makes sure he takes the time to answer the questions. When that person needs a lawyer or a friend asks for a referral, you probably can guess that Steve will be one of the first they consider calling.

Duffy Spencer, the social psychologist in Long Island, does two radio call-in shows about relationships and appears for five minutes, once a month, on News 12 Long Island, a twenty-four-hour cable news station. That five-minute shot, however, is repeated every hour during the entire day. More recently she made her cable network debut on the Lifetime channel. The exposure and credibility created from these shows are invaluable. She's been able to expand her career to a national level.

What to Say and How to Say It to the Media

You can generally contact the news media in one of two ways: press release or phone call.

The press release follows some very basic guidelines. Though there is some flexibility in the exact format, here is one to use as a guide.

1. Using your letterhead, on the upper right side put:

> FOR FURTHER INFORMATION CONTACT:
> The contact name (probably you)
> Your company name
> Address
> Phone number and fax number

Some of this information will appear on your letterhead but put it again. It takes out any ambiguity about whom to contact if the reporter has questions.

2. Skip a few lines, and at the left, in caps, put:

FOR IMMEDIATE RELEASE

3. Skip a few more lines, then, centered and boldface if you can, put your headline. The headline should be something that grabs the attention of the reporter. It will probably be rewritten, but you want something that in a few words tells what is the newsworthy item.

4. Skip a few lines, indent, and put your city in all caps followed by a couple of hyphens:

COLUMBUS, OHIO—

5. Immediately following those hyphens you start your release. The first sentence needs to contain much of the basic information about what you have: who, what, why, where, how, when. If it's not all covered in the first

sentence, then make sure it's covered in the first paragraph. In a press release the most important information is first, and additional information is presented in decreasing order of importance.

6. When you've finished, skip a few lines, then, to indicate the end of your press release, center some number signs:

#######

On the following page is what the press release looked like when we introduced our free telephone consulting to our "Profit Package." This release was sent to various trade journals.

In addition to this release we included a black-and-white 5″ × 7″ photo of the "Profit Package." This may sound much like an advertising ploy, but new product or service introductions are news, especially for trade journals. Most of the journals that printed this item actually included the phone number. Only several used the photo.

Your item may not get a full feature, but any exposure for a new service or product is worthwhile. In our case, none reprinted the press release in its entirety. But one publication conducted an interview about our entire concept because of this release.

When using a press release to set up an interview, it should be sent with a cover letter. It's best to keep this cover letter very brief. Stress that you thought this item would be of interest to the reporter's readers, listeners, or viewers, as the case may be.

Telephone. The telephone may work best if your item is a little more involved or very time-sensitive. The phone call also allows you to get immediate feedback. The reporter can instantly let you know if there's interest.

[On letterhead]

> FOR FURTHER INFORMATION CONTACT:
> Jeff Slutsky, President
> Streetfighter Marketing
> 467 Waterbury Court
> Gahanna, Ohio 43230
> (614) 337-7474   fax (614) 337-2233

FOR IMMEDIATE RELEASE

STREETFIGHTERS GIVE FREE PHONE HELP

COLUMBUS, OHIO—The "Streetfighters" have added free telephone consulting to their Streetfighters Profit Package, a complete audio and video training program that allows subscribers to call and brainstorm, ask questions, and help fine-tune the marketing and promotional ideas specifically to their needs.

"This is a $350 value that we're giving away as part of the package," according to Marc Slutsky, Vice-President of Streetfighter Marketing. He further went on to say, "This is a very inexpensive way for business people to take advantage of our program and get direct involvement."

The Profit Package currently contains one 1-hour videotape, two audiocassette albums consisting of a total of nine audiotapes and two workbooks, plus two books. The five items, which are available separately, sell in the Profit Package for $350 plus $7 shipping and handling. With the complete package the telephone consulting is provided free.

"The response has been very positive," according to Jeff Slutsky, the President. "It's not only a great way to help people get more direct ideas for their business, but helps us understand what's going on out in the field."

For information about the new Streetfighters Profit Package, call (800) 837-7355 or (614) 337-7474 in Ohio.

#######

When you call, it's very important that you stress the interest of the news item to the reporter's audience. When talking to a newspaper reporter, you say that this might be of interest to his "readers." A radio station wants news items of interest to their "listeners," and television newsrooms are concerned about their "viewers."

Keep the conversation low-key and not pushy. You are not a professional public relations person. Nor do you want to come off like a snake-oil salesperson. Rather, you're a member of the community with an item that might be of interest. It might sound something like this:

> "My name is Gloria Nelson with Nelson Construction here in Indianapolis and I've got a news item I'd like to run by you. Ummm . . . we're working on a building on the east side of town using a new construction material that is made up completely of recycled material. We got the idea at a conference we attended last year and I believe we're the first to use this new material in the area. I thought your viewers would find it interesting to see this side of the recycling process. Does this sound like something you might be interested in?"

In this hypothetical situation, notice the low-key presentation. The very important information is mentioned. She tied into a very topical issue, recycling, and at the end she asked to get the reporter's response to the idea. Gloria will know immediately if the reporter wants to do something with the story. If not, she has the option of contacting other TV stations. It's really that simple. Just make sure you've covered the basics:

1. You have something that is newsworthy.
2. You selected the appropriate media for your news item.

3. You've selected the appropriate contacts at the media.
4. You explain briefly and concisely what you have. Give all the main points in two to three sentences. Use an outline or script if you have to, but you do not want this to sound like you're reading it.
5. End with a question. Is this something they might be interested in? The only two acceptable answers are yes and no. Indecision can kill you.

When contacting the media, you need to figure out whom to contact. At the newspaper you can call and find out who the editor of a certain section is or you can find this out just by reading the bylines in the paper. Your other option is to call or send your release to the "City Desk" and it will be assigned.

When calling a television station, ask for the newsroom. For general news you might want to talk to the "producer" or "assignment editor." If the item is sports, you probably want to talk to the main sportscaster.

A radio station also has a news department. Just ask for the newsroom and just about anyone there can help. Many stations are pretty much a "rip and read" organization. They get news off the wire services and just read it on the air, so they might like to have something with a local flair.

Exclusive. If you have a big item of interest, it might help to offer the reporter an exclusive, which means you will give the story to no one else. For most situations you can offer an exclusive within that media. That is, you give the TV station a TV exclusive. This allows you to contact one radio station and a newspaper with the same item. Don't offer this unless it's necessary to get the story.

Organization. When you find or create a news opportunity, you want to have everything in place so you can easily contact the appropriate media. This means you need a list of the news media that you may want to contact regularly. The easiest way to do this is on computer. Using TeleMagic® software or other data base programs, you can create a news media list ready to spring into action.

Using this computer program, you can get phone numbers, addresses, and contacts immediately, just as you can for clients. This program will even dial the phone for you, print out mail-merged cover letters, and print the envelopes or labels. If you have a large calling list, you might want to divide up the work with others in your organization. When you find you're working from more than one computer, it becomes critical to network them using a local area network, or LAN, like Novell®, which is the one we use. We found that with Novell's version 2.2 for smaller users, the cost to network our computers was affordable and gave us dramatic improvement in our data base management. Of course we use both TeleMagic and Novell for much more than our news media list.

Media Sources. For developing media contacts in your local area start with the yellow pages. All the television, cable, radio, and print media will be listed, probably under "Advertising." For trade journals you can go to the library and look in the reference section for the SRDS (Standard Rate and Data Service). There's one for each major medium (i.e., trade journals, magazines, newspapers, radio, TV, mail lists). *Bacon's Publicity Checker* is a good directory for national exposure. You'll find a complete listing of publicity directories at the end of this chapter.

For the most part you should know the media and the specific shows or features you think would be of benefit to you. You don't want to send out press releases just to be sending them. Make sure you're not wasting the reporter's time with blatant commercials. When you do have something newsworthy, it will be that much more difficult to get attention (the boy who cried wolf syndrome).

Why the Press Wants Your Story

What is newsworthy? Tough question. It depends on the type of publication or media source, and sometimes it depends on what kind of news day they're having. If you catch them on a slow news day, you have a much greater chance of getting your item noticed.

On a local level or in trade journals very simple items usually get a blurb or mention. These include new staff, special industry awards or recognition, new products or services, expansion or consolidation, promotion, new ventures, acquisition of a major client, and national exposure. From the time I started my company I tried to get the local newspaper to do an article about us. They wouldn't even talk to me. I had been getting great exposure from papers all over the country. Finally, when I ended up on the front page of the second section of *The Wall Street Journal*, they came to me to do a feature story. The lead on that story was that a local business person was featured in the *Journal*. You really never know what it's going to take. Don't be afraid to ask.

Building Momentum With Publicity

Once you start getting publicity, at a certain level of exposure it becomes easier to get more. You become a recognized expert in your industry, so when a reporter needs an authority in your area, you're the likely one to contact.

Steve Trotter, the attorney from Fort Wayne mentioned

earlier, experienced this. A sportscaster at a local TV station also does some technical work on his radio talk show. They've known each other for years. When a reporter at the station needs to quote or interview an attorney, Steve's friend suggests they contact Steve. As a result they quote and interview him about various subjects related to his field.

Doug Hackbarth, of Broadview Florists, appeared in my first book, *Streetfighting*. He is a genius at getting free local publicity. Like Steve Trotter, Doug has his own radio show on Sundays, about plants. But for years, after a suggestion to a TV station, he has also had a weekly feature about plants and gardening. It's taped and on all three newscasts—noon, six, and eleven. Over the years he's had hundreds of thousands of dollars' worth of free exposure. When there was a major flood in the area, the newspaper contacted Doug about the effect on plants. On the front page of the paper was a picture of Doug in the greenhouse with floodwaters to his knees, watering plants from a hose that was elevated waist-high on tables. It was an interesting juxtaposition. He got this front-page exposure (which you couldn't buy if you wanted to) because his TV exposure kept him in the minds of the other reporters.

Avoiding and Dealing With Negative Press

Be careful with publicity. You have little control over the content of an article or news item. A reporter can write anything he or she wishes and often does. A clever editor can make you say things out of context. It probably won't happen often but it can happen.

Make your points clear. If there is anything you've said that can be misinterpreted, clarify. If you don't understand the reporter's question, ask it to be repeated. If it's still unclear, ask it to be restated in other words so you are clear. It's okay to say, "I'm not sure I understand your question."

There's No Such Thing as "Off the Record." Never, never, never say anything "off the record" to a reporter. There is no such thing as off the record. If you don't want it to appear on the front page of your paper, keep your mouth shut.

Avoid saying "No comment." It's too clichéd and people automatically think the worst. Soften it by saying, "I'm sorry but I can't comment on that right now." Or "I've been advised not to mention anything about this matter at this time." Keep answering the questions with "I'm sorry," suggesting that you can't answer.

Practicing Under Fire. The easiest interviews to control are live broadcasts. They can't edit, so you can say what you want to say. At the same time you want to prepare. To do so, write down every question you think the reporter will ask you. Especially write down the most embarrassing questions he or she can ask. Then think about an appropriate response. You can even get the aid of a local high school or junior college journalism class. Have them do a mock press conference to give you practice.

I got caught off guard once during a newspaper interview. This miniature Mike Wallace was out to get me for some reason. Had I sensed what she was up to, I might have handled the interview differently. Regardless, I shared some stories that described the "Streetfighter's attitude." One story concerned the more clever and effective ways restaurants got new customers:

Many years ago in the Midwest there was a fun restaurant. It was very successful. The problem was that Tuesday sales were always weak. The manager tried every crazy promotion to build Tuesdays, but nothing would work.

One day he's thumbing through the local phone book and by chance comes across a person with the name of John Wayne. He calls up the local John Wayne and tells him that his name was selected at random out of the local phone book. He just won a dinner for two next Tuesday night at eight. John was ecstatic. He had never won anything before in his life. He thanked the manager and said that he and his wife would be there at eight.

The next day a huge banner goes out in front of the restaurant that read: "John Wayne to dine here next Tuesday!" Tuesday rolls around, normally a totally dead day, and he has the busiest happy hour in the history of the restaurant. By six there was a waiting line for dinner. By seven the waiting line was out the front door. People were waiting in line with autograph books, eight-by-ten glossies, cameras. By a quarter till eight, the state police came out to direct traffic, it was so backed up. Inside it was packed. Total pandemonium. You barely could hear yourself think.

Eight o'clock and there's an announcement over the loud speaker. "Ladies and gentlemen . . . Mr. and Mrs. John Wayne."

Silence.

Now, John has no idea what's going on. Finally everyone realized what had happened. They broke out laughing. They ushered John to his seat. They were even asking him for his autograph.

When I tell this story in my speech, I use it as an example of knowing when you're crossing over the line. This idea, even for a crazy restaurant, is too risky. It could have just as easily backfired. But I didn't mention this part of it to the reporter.

The interview went great. But when I saw the article, I couldn't believe it. She ripped me apart. Said I was teaching people how to deceive consumers. You have to be very, very careful when talking to a reporter. From that time forward, I made sure that they understood my points. Oddly enough I got a few clients from the article. But the point is, leave nothing to chance and learn from mistakes. This story notwithstanding, you'll find that publicity, when done properly, can be one of your most effective marketing tools for getting new clients.

Publicity Resource Guide

Here is a list of directories that can be helpful in your publicity efforts. Some of these can be found in your local library.

Bacon's Media Alerts
Bacon's Publicity Checker
Bacon's Radio/TV Directory
    Bacon's Publishing Company
    332 S. Michigan Ave.
    Chicago, IL 60611
    (312) 922-2400

Cable Contacts
Radio Contacts
Syndicated Columnists Directory
TV News Contacts
Television Contacts
    BPI Communications, Inc.
    1515 Broadway
    New York, NY 10036
    (212) 536-5260

Directory American Society of Journalists
and Authors 1991

> American Society of Journalists and Authors, Inc.
> 1501 Broadway, Ste. 1907
> New York, NY 10036
> (212) 997-0947; fax 768-7414

Feature News Publicity Outlets
National Radio Publicity Outlets

> Resource Media, Inc.
> Box 307
> Kent, CT 06757
> (800) 441-3839

Metro California Media
New York Publicity Outlet

> Public Relations Plus, Inc.
> P.O. Drawer 1197
> New Milford, CT 06776
> (800) 999-8448

Standard Periodical Directory

> Oxbridge Communications
> 150 Fifth Ave., Ste. 301
> New York, NY 10011
> (212) 741-0231

Business Publications Rates and Data
Community Publications Rates and Data
Consumer Magazines and Agri-Media Rates and Data
Direct Mail Lists Rates and Data
Hispanic Media and Markets
Newspaper Rates and Data
Spot Radio Rates and Data

Spot Television Rates and Data
   Standard Rate and Data Service
   3004 Glenview Rd.
   Wilmette, IL 60091
   (708) 441-2339

CHAPTER 6

Client Contacts Through Community Commitment

David owns a life insurance company specializing in serving well-off and wealthy clients. He is very involved in his temple, and when the Board of Directors was concerned about the long-term financial stability of his congregation, he came to them with a creative solution to their problem.

His company created a special life insurance policy, with the temple as the beneficiary. Their goal was eventually to raise $1 million. Each individual policy would have a $10,000 payout at death. This meant he needed to sell one hundred of these policies to reach the million-dollar goal. The cost of the policy ranged from $119 per year to $430 per year for eleven years. The cost of premiums was based on the policyholder's age. David kicked it off by buying the first ten units. He then listed the most generous congregants and suggested they, too, buy ten units each. His objective was to get the congregation's "heavy hitters" to cover half the million-dollar goal.

This program, from the insurance person's point of view, is not profitable. It's a lot of work for very little commission. Yet it puts him in front of many potential clients talking about his product and gathering valuable information. The contacts and opportunity to meet with them make this a brilliant approach that is also an immense contribution to this cause. Everybody wins.

Commitment in your local or industry community helps you network with many of your potential clients effectively and cheaply. In this chapter you'll discover how to take advantage of these opportunities while at the same time avoiding costly mistakes.

High Visibility With Low Liability

A primary concept of community commitment that I wrote about in *Streetfighting* is "high visibility with low liability." This means that you want a lot of exposure, not to mention paying clients, for your effort, but you want it using little money or time. David's insurance program was a good example of this idea. Another example of this approach is illustrated in the following excerpt from *Streetfighting*:

Jack owns and operates a chain of successful quick print shops. He was approached by a pro/amateur celebrity golf tournament. This major event raises money for charity every year. The charity people wanted Jack to be a sponsor in the event. The cost of sponsorship was $750 that got your name in the program book and on a plaque on the eighteenth hole along with nineteen other sponsors. Not much exposure for your $750.

He said that this was such a worthy cause that he wanted to do something very special. Jack offered to put up a $10,000 cash prize for the first golfer to get a hole in one on the ninth hole; $5,000 would go to the golfer and $5,000 donated to the charity. They were ecstatic. This added a whole new dimension to the tournament and he instantly received tens of thousands of dollars' worth of free news media exposure. He was an instant hero.

He wasn't worried about the risk because he took out an insurance policy through Lloyds of London protecting him against someone scoring the hole in one. The funny thing about it was that the cost of the policy was $450—$300 less than the sponsorship, yet he totally dominated the tournament.

Jack's offer was so successful that he continued to sponsor the hole-in-one contest, and a few years later, someone got it! Of course the follow-up publicity was tremendous.

When Is Enough Too Tough?

An important concept in community commitment is to provide valuable service to a group that's important to you from a business standpoint. Ideally this contribution or service that you provide should directly or indirectly bring you new clients. If it doesn't, the effort is worthless from a marketing standpoint.

You don't necessarily have to get involved to the degree of the two examples just mentioned. Sometimes just being an active member of an organization helps you get exposed to potential clients. Obviously you need to join the right organizations. Before joining any group for business reasons, go as a guest as often as is allowed and get to know the members. See if a significant number of the members fall into your target group of potential clients.

Joining a trade organization can't do this for you. It's a great place to hone your skills and perhaps meet suppliers, but often it's a lousy place to make business contacts. These organizations are filled with your competitors, so be careful. The organization to join is one with few of your competitors but many potential clients.

Once you join such an organization, you'll need some visibility, but first it's a good idea just to feel your way around for a while. Get to know some people and some of the politics of the organization. If you come on too strong and too soon, you'll turn off many of your potential clients.

You also want to take the "get acquainted" time to figure the structure of the organization: which committees can put you in close contact with the right people for the least amount of effort. It takes a little time to figure this out, but putting a little research and reconnaissance time in at first can reap you big rewards later.

Don't feel that every group you join has to lead to business. If there is an organization or cause that you feel strongly about, by all means participate. And if that organization has minimal business potential, that's fine. Just don't expect your involvement in this organization to yield business and don't think of it as marketing. Joining an organization because you want to for personal reasons might give you a false sense of security when looking at your general marketing effort.

Country clubs are fine if that's where your potential clients are or if it is the type of environment you want for entertaining your clients. You want a club that portrays the right image for your goals.

If you're looking for a high-end clientele, you'll find better opportunities getting involved with organizations like the symphony, theater, museums, ballet, opera, and certain causes sponsored by hospitals.

To get an idea of the causes that could help you the most, look at the segment of your client list you would most like to clone. Then when you see these particular clients, you probe a little to discover the organizations and nonprofit groups they support. Often there will be plaques, awards, photos, or other mementos displayed in their office or home. When reading your local newspaper, a client's name may be mentioned as a participant in a certain cause.

You'll probably find that they love to talk about it, so ask questions and listen. Learn why they got involved and how they won the award. It's not only a good stroke but you'll uncover valuable information about your client and his or her peers.

Artfully Refusing Donation Solicitation

We're often asked to donate money to worthy causes. If a good client calls you and wants you to buy raffle tickets or an ad in a program book for some worthy cause, you probably should do it. Just buy the smallest amount necessary to keep the client happy.

If a client's kid calls for the same thing, you'll probably have to buy it as well. Don't expect a return on investment. You've thrown away that marketing money but if you turned down the request, it might cause hard feelings. A loss of goodwill with that client is not good. Is it worth it? If the client calls and wants a $10,000 donation and only generates $5,000 in fees, you have an easy decision to make. In most situations, though, you'll find that they'll ask for a nominal donation.

Occasionally you'll get a request from someone on the phone that goes like this:

> "Hey, Jeff, how you doin' today? Me and the boys down here at the fire station were just talking about you last week. We're gettin' ready to put t'gether our program book again this year and were wond'rin' if'n we can count on your support again this year?"

You'll notice a few things about these phone calls. First, they call you by your first name. Then they always ask how you are as if they really cared. Lastly they always want your support "again this year," though you never gave it to them last year!

What's probably happening is that you're getting a telemarketing call from a boiler-room operation based in a different state. Only a fraction of the money they make goes to the charity. If it is in fact a telemarketing operation, you have no problem in politely saying, "Thanks anyway, but I'm not interested." Then hang up.

You must make sure that it is not a legitimate local group making the call before you hang up. You want to maintain a good-guy image in your community. To figure out if it is a telemarketing pitch, you can respond with:

> "You know, that sounds just like the type of worthy cause we like to support here at our company. I need to run this by my partner [boss, supervisor, etc.] and get their permission. Give me a number where I can get back to you."

Most of the time they can't take an inbound call and won't give you a number. They'll tell you they'll call back. Be firm. Tell them you'll be in and out and they can't get in touch with you. Most of the time, out of frustration, they'll just hang up on you and won't call back.

We had a client once that had a great way of getting rid of these people. As soon as he heard, "Hey, Joe, how you doing today?" he could safely assume that it was a telemarketing pitch. As soon as they asked him how he was, he'd go into his presentation, using a very upset voice:

> "I'm awful. My wife just left me for another man.
> Three employees showed up late and one not at all.
> And to top it off, my daughter just ran off with some
> biker. Now what the hell do you want?"

About halfway through the call you should hear a click.

Every once in a while you do get a legitimate call from a local person. So you might try the following response. First listen to the presentation all the way through, then say:

> "You know, that sounds like just the type of worthy cause
> we here at our company like to support. But here's
> my problem. Every year we put away a budget for
> just such worthy causes. Unfortunately this year's budget
> is all used up. But if you get back to us a little earlier
> next year, I'm sure we can work something out. Fair
> enough?"

Now, you're not rejecting them . . . it's just that their timing is a little off. Next year rolls around. Committees change. People move in and out of town. And someone new approaches you. How do you handle it? See the paragraph above!

Social Events: Opportunities Only for the Nonobnoxious

Whether going to a meeting or a cocktail party, you must always keep your eyes open and ears to the ground for client opportunities.

Once my father-in-law took me to a social event. It was a fun night called "Boys Night Out." Great food and entertainment. As it turns out, I'm seated next to the owner of a very successful insurance agency in town. One of his agents sold me a policy when my daughter was born. We got on the subject of marketing, and within a half an hour he insisted that he hire me. I did not go to that event thinking about getting a new client. I wasn't really trying to sell him on the idea of using our services. But through the conversation, he was sharing some problems he had, and I just happened to have the solutions.

PREPARING FOR SOCIAL EVENTS

Before going to any social gathering be prepared. Many people, especially ones that have little sales experience, have difficulty meeting new people unless properly introduced. Shyness is a serious problem when getting clients. This is a problem I have to deal with every day.

Many people can't believe that I'm shy, but I have a terrible time at social events. I really have to force myself to meet new people. I have no problem at all speaking before a group of over a thousand, but at a party you'll often find me in the corner nursing a drink and pretending like I'm really interested in the wallpaper. To help me get over this, I've worked with Susan RoAne, a San Francisco-based speaker and author of the best-seller *How to Work a*

Room. She offers these ten simple tips for getting the most out of any business social event:[23]

1. Get the right attitude. If you think to yourself you're going to have a lousy time, you will. Though it's business, go with the attitude of having a good time.

2. Prepare your introduction. After your name and company, have a brief statement ready describing what you do. Add something that makes what you do sound interesting. Rehearse your statement so it doesn't sound like you've memorized it verbatim, like a flight attendant going through safety procedures. (You might want to review the "benefit statement." See page 159.)

3. Prepare conversation starters. You do this by being well read. Read your local newspaper. Read the sports, business, and general news. It gives you something to talk about. Even if you're not a sports fan, for example, it's good to know if something special has happened. Be aware of any news about major corporations in your area. Read the event sponsor's publications. If your local Chamber of Commerce is the sponsor, for example, be sure to read their latest newsletter. Being at this event is something you do have in common.

4. Don't expect to close sales but rather look for possible leads or even people with whom to network. All your time doesn't have to be spent with someone you think can buy what you have. You might find someone who could be a source of referrals down the road. It always pays to be nice and attentive. You never know where that person will end up in ten years.

5. Bring plenty of business cards. Don't bring

---

[23]*How to Work a Room*, by Susan RoAne (New York: Warner Books, 1989). Also available on audiocassette by Audio Renaissance.

brochures or sales material. It's inappropriate and too pushy.

6. Make eye contact. When you're talking to someone, give that person your complete attention. It's really annoying to have someone talk to you while they're busy looking around for their next move.

7. Be smart about alcohol, food, gum, and smoking. Limit your alcohol intake. Nurse a drink or two during the evening. You want to keep your wits about you. Keep your drink in your left hand to avoid ice-cold handshakes. If you're hungry, hit the buffet when you first get there, then keep your hands clean and free for meeting people. If you smoke, you should consider avoiding it at these meetings. You're likely to offend a significant number of people. If you absolutely must, leave, smoke, then return. If you chew gum, it should only be done if not noticeable. If it is noticeable, you might as well wear it on your nose. And don't use breath spray during the event. Too obvious. A breath mint is subtle and effective.

8. Be careful with humor. It's too easy to offend someone. Especially avoid ethnic or sexual innuendo. Even if someone laughs on the outside, you don't know if you've hurt or offended him or her on the inside. It's not worth the risk.

9. Follow up. If there's someone you met that you think is worth following up, do so and do it quickly. You should probably call within a few days of the event. The longer you wait, the less likely they'll remember you.

10. If you can't remember the name of someone you've met before, admit it. It's acceptable to admit a lapse in memory. It's bothersome if you try to fake it. By the same token, reintroduce yourself by name with those you've met before. Assume that they don't remember. If you keep them from getting embarrassed, you'll develop a much stronger rapport.

The skill to remember names and faces can be learned and can be a big advantage. Remembering people's names is a powerful marketing tool, but unfortunately very few of us have the ability to do it. One of the biggest problems about going to social events is that you're introduced to many people throughout the evening. Most of us forget their names almost immediately. By learning how to remember names and faces you can have an advantage. People always appreciate having their names remembered. It shows that you care.

There are some programs out there that teach you to do this. One is an audio album entitled *On Your Way to Remembering Names & Faces*, by Bob Burg.[24] In his course he teaches professionals how to use imagery and association to make it easier to link a person's name with his face as well as his profession or work. Like any new skill, it takes time and effort but is one that I feel will pay you dividends in the future.

---

[24]*On Your Way to Remembering Names & Faces*, by Bob Burg. ©Bob Burg's Memory Unlimited, P.O. Box 7002, Jupiter, FL 33468. (800) 726-3667.

CHAPTER 7

Getting More From Direct Mail

One day I received a letter selling a payroll service from ADT. It came in a standard envelope. I often read my junk mail, so I opened it. It immediately caught my attention. There was a penny taped to the top of the letter. It opened up with "Just One Penny," then the salutation.

The first line of the letter repeated this announcement. The letter went on to say that if your payroll is off by just one penny, it could cause you big problems with the IRS. I didn't call but I did remember the letter. When the author of that letter followed up a week later, I did take his phone call. Had it been a cold call without the letter, I probably would not have.

This is an exception. I feel that usually you are better off calling first, then sending out mail. But sales letters can help you build your business. Direct mail allows you to target a very specific group of people. You can mail to your existing clients or to potential clients. There are a variety of approaches one can use with direct mail. For getting clients, the most common are sales letters and newsletters.

Getting the Envelope Opened

Most junk mail ends up in the trash unread. The envelopes aren't even opened. When using mail, look for ways to get the prospective client to, at the very least, open the envelope. Here are some hints for envelopes:

1. An address printed or typed directly on the envelope gets better response than an address label. Handwritten addresses do even better. Having the person's name is better than "Occupant" or title only.

2. First class usually does better than third-class bulk mail. There is a big difference in cost. With third class you have to mail at least two hundred pieces. You can now get a stamp for third class instead of printing a permit, which makes it look a little more like first class.

3. A stamp gets more attention than a meter. The more stamps the better. Use big, colorful commemorative stamps. It makes it look less like junk mail.

4. Window envelopes seem to pull better. Double windows even better yet. It looks like a bill or invoice and is more likely to get opened.

5. Look for ways to make impact while maintaining professionalism. You're not selling magazine subscriptions, so avoid the gaudy stuff.

Writing a More Effective Letter

You don't have to get fancy to get results. Just stick to some basic ideas.

1. The "P.S." is the first item to be read. Make sure that your P.S. is designed to cause enough interest to get the reader to want to read the letter. When your letter is first opened, most people will look to see who sent it. Then they notice the P.S. Consider using something like, "Dave Jones of ABC Company told us that this program saved them 41%." The reader asks him- or herself, who is Jones and how did they save 41%? It's just compelling enough to get the reader's interest.

2. The first sentence is your headline. You need strong benefit immediately. "You can save as much as 41% on the cost of your payroll service" hits the reader right between the eyes with benefit. Notice that I've used 41% and not 40%. Don't round off. Be reasonably exact. 41.3% is too exact. Balance.

3. Indent your paragraphs. They're easier to read. And skip a line between paragraphs.

4. Use a ragged right margin. Even if your letters are done on a word processor and laser printer, you don't want them to look that way. A justified right margin automatically makes your letters look like they're run on a computer. That immediately suggests to the reader that it's a mass mailing. Readers want mail directed specifically to their needs. And use a print style, like "courier," that looks like a typewriter, not a computer.

5. If possible, hand-sign the letters. Use blue ink so the reader knows it's not a printed copy of your signature.

6. Keep it short, but say everything you need to say. As long as you are presenting benefits to the reader, they'll continue to read.

7. At the end, give a call to action. Have them call you or send back a business reply postcard for follow-up. You must ask them to do something or they won't.

Frequency. Frequency is another factor for success. A onetime mailing often falls short. A prospective client who doesn't know you might not pay attention to your letter at first. But if that letter comes repeatedly, you stand a better chance. You can send the same letter to the same address three or four times over two to three months.

Sometimes timing is the key to success. Send your letter at regular intervals, say quarterly. If a client suddenly needs your services, you've made impact when they're making a decision. The frequency approach might be more effective when done with a newsletter.

List Quality. The higher the quality of your mailing list, the better the response. If you know who you want to put on your list, that's helpful. But you can buy lists from list brokers. They're broken down by industry category called SIC codes. To find what mail lists are available, visit your local library's reference section for the SRDS (Standard Rate and Data Service) for mail lists. (See page 104.)

To maintain a high-quality list, you might consider mailing first-class once a year. If you're mailing bulk, you won't get address changes returned to you. With first class you will.

Testing to Fine-tune

The beauty about direct mail is that you can test everything. Before mailing a couple thousand pieces, send out a few hundred to see the response. A 3 to 5 percent response rate in direct mail is considered good. Your response rate is greatly dependent upon the quality of your mailing list. A response rate is the percentage of people who took the desired action. It doesn't mean they'll automatically become your clients. Your mail can only cause them to call, write, or visit you.

When testing, test only one element at a time. Simple variables worth testing include:

1. Third class versus first class
2. Two different P.S.'s
3. Two different opening sentences
4. Adding a business reply postcard
5. Free offer for quick action

The possibilities are endless. Only through testing, over time, will you begin to get an idea of what gets you the best response. Every time you change an element in a direct-mail piece, it can affect the results. To understand which elements work better, you can't change more than one variable for each test.

To know which version is working best, you need a tracking device. This is a special extension number added to your phone number or a special suite number to your address. Each version of your letter offers a different extension and suite number. When the prospect replies, the suite number on the address or the extension they give when asked lets you know which version they have. This same technique can be used with any form of advertising or marketing.

The 25 Percent Response Mailer

One of the biggest successes we've heard in direct mail was used by a quick printer. She was attending a convention for printers in Las Vegas. While she was there she bought four hundred picture postcards of Las Vegas. When she returned home to her small community, she printed the reverse side of these postcards with "Don't Gamble on Your Printing Needs." She then told the recipients to bring the postcard in for a 10 percent discount on their next printing order.

To create the mailing list, she went through the boldface listings in the white pages of her local phone book. She'd check off names of companies she didn't recognize as already being her customers. Her kids, after school, hand-addressed the postcards.

She received one hundred back. That's a 25 percent return, which is unheard-of! Most people toss out junk mail right away. They won't even open the envelope. But if you get a picture postcard from Las Vegas, you're at least going to see who it's from. That's half the battle. She then did a very clever job using a headline that tied in with the picture on the card.

One additional benefit from a postcard mailing is that the cost of postage is much lower than for a letter.

Somers White, a speaking colleague of ours based in Phoenix, takes his mailing list with him when he travels overseas. His clients receive postcards from such places as China. It makes a great impact and shows your clients that you're thinking about them. This is of particular interest if the trip is somehow tied into business.

Sending a postcard mailing to clients from some exotic place is a benefit if you're there attending a conference to learn how to do what you do better. Of course, you want to make sure that if you use this approach, the note on the card is appropriate for that client. You might make a negative impression if a client sees that you're traveling all over the world instead of taking care of him. Think it through.

A custom postcard is also a great way to handle your informal correspondence. For dropping a quick note to someone on your list it's ideal, since the cost is so low.

There's less postage and no envelope. And you should handwrite it (legibly), which saves on secretarial time.

How to Use a Free Gift to Get Attention

We've had very little luck with standard direct-mail efforts, with one exception. We tried mailing out brochures and letters to prospective clients but got little if any response. So we tested something. We took our book *Streetfighting* and mailed it as part of our direct-mail campaign. At that time this was our only book. We figured it was sacrilegious to throw away a book. We would mail out five a day along with a cover letter. Since it was a book, we could mail it out at the book rate, which saved on some postage.

Our goal was to mail out a total of three hundred books to upper management of companies we wanted as our clients. This was obviously a very selective list. Every day five more would go out. It worked. We started getting calls from prospective clients. Some wanted to buy more copies of the book. Others wanted to hire us for speaking and consulting. It really helped to get things moving for us.

There was even a residual benefit beyond the clients calling us directly as a result of the book mailing. Our salespeople calling them had a much easier time getting through. The book mailing gave us awareness and credibility prior to the sales calls.

When our second book was released, *Street Smart Marketing*, part of the marketing program with the publisher was to mail a copy to the CEOs of major companies. Only about half the Fortune 500 would have interest in this book. Then we compiled another 250 names of other larger corporations who we felt would find the information valuable.

This time the publisher mailed the books. The book has done well, in part due to this exposure. We've noticed some calls for our services from companies on that list. Where it has been very valuable to us is when our salespeople make calls on these companies. Often the contact is familiar with us from the book. It was mailed to the CEO or VP of Marketing but then sent down a few levels.

You might look at mailing a free gift. This can be costly, but if done to a very targeted group, can provide a big payback. There are four guidelines you should follow when considering using the more expensive "free gift" approach to your direct mail.

1. The free gift must be valuable enough so it won't be tossed at first sight.
2. The free gift must be affordable enough to allow you to take the risk of using it in a selected mailing.
3. The free gift must be something your prospects want.
4. The free gift should directly relate to or reinforce your products and services.

A creative banker on the East Coast used to shrink-wrap his business cards with a Susan B. Anthony dollar. He'd pass them out to prospective clients and enclose them in mailings. It got attention and prospects kept them.[25]

Craig Adler is a sales rep for German Village Travel in

---

[25]From *The Great Brain Robbery*, by Murray Raphel and Ray Considine. Self-published. Gordon's Alley, Atlantic City, N.J.

Ohio. When making sales calls he'll get a couple of business cards from the prospect. In his follow-up thank-you letter he enclosed a laminated luggage tag encasing the prospect's business cards.

Gene Hameroff published a booklet entitled *33 One Liners to Improve Your Ad Agency.* With some classified advertising in advertising trade journals, prospective agency clients can send away for a free copy. It's then followed up by one of his salespeople later.

Nuances for Avoiding the Newsletter Nuisance

Newsletters are a major undertaking because it is something that is done regularly. Think carefully before launching headfirst into developing and publishing a newsletter.

Newsletter Service. The easiest way to get a newsletter is to buy one "boilerplate." There may be companies who sell such a service in your industry. Some industries have companies that write and produce the newsletter for you. You then have a page or two in the prewritten piece to add your own articles or ads. You also have your name on the cover, so it looks like the newsletter comes from you and you write it. Make sure that the information they provide is what you want to provide your clients and prospects. You pay for this service but it does relieve much of the burden from you.

Self-published Newsletters. If you choose to write and produce your own newsletter, consider publishing it as a special edition. In this way you're not stuck having to come out with a monthly, bimonthly, or quarterly newsletter if you don't want to. Just give it an issue number and not a date. On the other hand, frequency, while an operational negative, is a marketing advantage. The repetition of newsletters makes it a great way to stay in touch with your clients regularly.

Should you decide to do your own newsletter, I'd suggest you start out simple. If you want to expand, then work your way up to a more involved piece after you've had some experience with it. Consider starting with just a single sheet of paper, front and back. Have a quality masthead or banner designed and printed on an attractive paper that reproduces well. You can have the masthead done in a couple of colors and printed in one run to save money.

The typical formats for newsletters are:

8½" × 11", one fold, two panels
8½" × 14", single fold, four panels
11" × 17", single fold, four panels
11" × 17" with 8½" × 11" insert,
single fold, six panels

You can then use any combination of 11 × 17s for an additional four panels or 8½ × 11 for two more panels.

Some newsletters are being printed as tabloids on newsprint. This can be cost-effective but make sure you are presenting an appropriate image for you.

Printing Tips on Saving You Tons of Money

If you plan to run, let's say, a quarterly 8½" × 11" newsletter that goes out to 1,000 people, you'll need 4,000 pieces of newsletter paper for the year. Since the masthead doesn't change, get 4,500 masthead pieces with additional colors, foil, embossing, or other more expensive processes done at once. This gives you economies of scale. Then when you print a particular issue, simply give the typewritten copy to your printer. Typewriter print is acceptable for a newsletter, since it should be news that's "hot off the press."

Layout and Design. If you have a laser printer and word processing software like WordPerfect and the help of Rick Sullivan, author of *Advanced WordPerfect*,[26] you can produce a professional-looking piece inexpensively. Your printer runs the black copy on front and back. Gang-running your masthead drastically reduces printing costs compared to doing the same job four different times.

Notice that in the example I suggest printing 4,500 pieces of masthead though you only need 4,000 for the year. That's because in reality you'll have paper jams, typos, and other situations that might eat up the more expensive reprinted masthead. Better to have a little too much than not enough. The cost difference from 4,000 to even 6,000 is not that much more.

Newsletter Content. Keep the articles short and easy to read. Don't use a lot of your industry's technical jargon. It's perfectly acceptable to quote or paraphrase your trade journals if that information is usable to your clients. Be sure to state sources because it not only is the right thing to do, it makes you out to be more credible.

You can even ask some of your peers (preferably noncompetitive) to submit articles. And similarly, you may not wish to publish your own newsletter, but you can be a contributor to someone else's.

Copies of your newsletter or newsletter articles can go into your portfolio and marketing material. They're also mailed out to your clients and prospective clients. By modifying the copy of your newsletter, is it possible to adapt it to a wider target audience of benefit?

---

[26]*Advanced WordPerfect 5.0/5.1*, by Rick Sullivan (Cincinnati: South-Western Publishing Co., 1991).

The VOCA Corporation, one of the nation's leading providers of residential services for people with mental retardation, took a second look at their newsletter, which was geared toward their employees. With some slight changes, the same success stories used in the newsletter interested other important groups, including the government officials responsible for hiring their company. For just the cost of adding a few more hundred to the mailing list, their newsletter helps them share success stories with an existing and potential client base.

CHAPTER 8

How to Get All the Information You Need to Get Client Commitment

I remember a very unhappy experience when I went shopping for a new car. The odd thing was that after the experience I discovered I was not alone. Hank Tressler in his book *No Bull Selling* relates a similar experience. At the time, I was driving a big luxury car and thought it was time to buy a sports car. A close friend of mine had a very nice sports car and let me drive it a couple times. I soon decided that the one thing I wanted most out of life was to drive fast and look cool.

I started shopping around at a number of dealerships and every time the same thing happened. Some guy in a plaid polyester sport coat comes out, shakes my hand, pops the hood on the car to show me the engine, and then starts talking about how much money he can save me. There I am, staring underneath the hood of these cars. I have no idea how an engine works. I look at all these tubes and wires and fans and belts and it means absolutely nothing to me. The salesman is going on and on about cams and liters and ratios and injection things. I have no idea what he is talking about. All I want is to drive fast and look cool.

Finally at one of the places I went to, a salesman comes out while I am looking over a particular car. It was hot. But what captured my attention was that he did not pop the hood. Instead he asked me a question: "I see you're interested in one of our most popular cars. Let me ask you, what is it about this car that grabbed your attention?"

He was showing interest in me. I got a little excited and responded, "My buddy has one very similar to this and he let me drive it. I couldn't believe how fast it was and how well it handled."

"You like to drive fast?"

"Oh, yeah."

"I had this one out the other day and cranked it up to ninety. Then I shifted into second. Is that fast enough for you?"

"Wow."

"Not only that, whenever I take this car out, everybody thinks I'm cool."

"I'll take it!"

He had me. I sold me what I wanted. He found out my hot buttons. I looked at many comparable cars for weeks, but no one offered the solution to my problem, drive fast and look cool. Even so he would not sell me that car. I could not believe it. Instead he comes back with, "Listen. You do not want this car and I'll tell you why. For three thousand more I can get you a sticker on the back that says 'turbo.'"

"What's it do?"

"I don't know, but you can drive faster and look cooler!"

"I'll take it!"

And he was absolutely right. Everywhere I went everyone noticed the little turbo sticker. I thought turbo was a type of fish. I did not know. But he knew what I wanted to buy and sold it to me. And I felt great about my decision. I knew that this car, with turbo, is what I really wanted all along.

I was a little heartbroken about six months later. I discovered that my turbo sticker had fallen off. I'll get a new one, you can be sure of that.

The Secret of Getting What You Want

If "marketing" and "advertising" are scary terms, then "sales" is horrifying! Yet everyone is a salesperson whether he or she realizes it or not. Unfortunately sales brings to mind pushy people involved in a scam. Sometimes that's true. Yet sales is one of the most important skills there is. Without it nothing gets done.

Up till now, I've avoided the word "sales." It's offensive to many, especially those in the profession. But sales is nothing more than having the communication skill needed to get a client to understand the value of what you have. It's a skill that is important in our business as well as our everyday life. Everything is a sale. When you want your kid to mow the grass or pick up his or her room . . . that's a sale. When he wants to borrow the car, that's a sale. When you're debating which TV show to watch or where to go to dinner, that's a sale.

How to Control Every Conversation

The truth of the matter is that most people in sales don't know how to sell. They haven't mastered the one very simple yet effective concept in sales, according to Bill Bishop: *The person asking the questions controls the conversation.*

There are several reasons for this. First, when you are asking a question, it forces the other person to pay attention to you. If you merely talk, the listener's mind can wander and think about other things. But the minute you say, "Let me ask you this..." the listener must pay attention because a response will be required. It is an automatic reflex.

Second, I learned from a sales trainer years ago that a person can speak at about 250 words a minute while a person who is listening can think at about 1,200 words a minute. Of course these are rough averages. I have some friends in New York who talk at 350 words a minute with gusts of up to 400. And my friends in the South talk about 125. Yet you do think about five to six times as fast as you talk. So when you're doing all the talking to a prospect, he or she has a great deal more time to figure reasons not to work with you. By you asking the questions and letting the prospect do the talking, you have the advantage of thinking many times faster than the prospect.

Third, when you ask a question, you show compassion and concern for the needs of the prospective client. It helps you build rapport. Try this: The next time you go to a cocktail party play a game of trying to keep the other person talking as much as possible. Listen and show concern. Ask questions and turn it back over to the other person. You'll soon be known as a great conversationalist, even though you said very little.

Perhaps the most important aspect of asking questions is that it allows you to get valuable information from the prospect. You can discover your prospect's needs. People love to talk about themselves, so let them, and in the process, gather all the other information you can.

Information gathering is the secret. The more you know, the better off you are. And you can find all you need to know by simply asking and listening.

The Hot Potato Exercise. To control the conversation simply be the last person to ask the question. Eventually the client will tell you exactly what he or she needs in order to work with you. Following with a question is not a natural skill. It's something you have to practice. In our seminars we do an exercise to help people learn this skill. It's called "hot potato." Get a partner. Pick a subject, any subject. Make it a fun topic. Then one person begins by asking a question. The second person responds by answering that question briefly, then following up with his or her own question. Then the first person does the same. This goes back and forth till one person does not follow up with a question. That's the buyer.

The World's Best Salespeople

The best salespeople in the world aren't in life insurance, nor are they selling cars. The best salespeople in the world are children. I had an opportunity to witness what is perhaps one of the best sales presentations of all time last summer. We had some friends over for a barbecue. About a half hour before dinner their five-year-old daughter wanted to go out and play with some other kids in the neighborhood. She used expert sales technique to do it. First she asked a closing question. That is a question that asks for a decision.

"Can I go out and play?"

"No. Dinner will be ready soon," the mother responded.

"Why?" the five-year-old asked.

"Because," the mother responded.

At this point notice that the five-year-old is the one asking the questions. The child is in control. Then she came back with "But because why?"

"Because I said so," Mom retorted.

"But because why?" the little girl asked, unyielding.

"Because I'm the mommy!" Mom responded shortly.

This went on for a few more minutes. I counted the exchanges as this went on for a total of sixteen times. The little girl just kept at it. Every time she responded with a question, the mother would get more and more frustrated. Finally after the sixteenth objection Mom yelled back, "Okay already! Get the hell out and come back in a half hour!"

Sale closed.

Now, how does a five-year-old know that two of the most important ideas in getting what you want are asking and persistence? I was amazed. This was textbook sales. I discovered why a few months later. I was buying a book to read to my daughter, Amanda. As I read the book I started paying attention to story line. Then it hit me. It's the books we read our children that teach them how to be such great salespeople. The book I bought for Amanda was *Green Eggs and Ham,* by Dr. Seuss.[27]

This book has two main characters. The first is a salesman by the name of Sam-I-Am. He has a prospect: the Cat in the Hat. Sam has a new product introduction. He's trying to get the Cat to try this new product: Green Eggs and Ham. The Cat wants nothing to do with this new product. But Sam keeps using a sales technique

---

[27]*Green Eggs and Ham,* by Dr. Seuss. Copyright 1960 by Theodor S. Geisel and Audrey S. Geisel. Beginner Books, a division of Random House.

called the "choice close." This is when you give the prospect the choice between two positive responses, like "Would you like it delivered Tuesday or Wednesday?" Despite the choice, the sale is made.

This technique is a little dated. Sam uses it repeatedly on the Cat: "Would you eat them here or there?"

The Cat objects, "I would not eat them here or there. I would not eat them anywhere. I do not like Green Eggs and Ham. I do not like them, Sam-I-Am."

Major objection. Most people would quit. Not Sam. Comes back with another choice close: "Would you eat them in a house? Would you eat them with a mouse?"

The Cat responds with "I would not eat them in a house. I would not eat them with a mouse. I would not eat them here or there. I would not eat them anywhere. I do not like Green Eggs and Ham. I do not like them, Sam-I-Am."

Major objection. Most people would quit. Not Sam. Comes back with another and another and another. Sixteen times he does this! Finally at the end the Cat breaks down and says that if Sam would just leave him alone and not bother him anymore he would try it. (Of course he rhymed it a little better than that.)

Then he tries this new product. The Cat loves it. He's going to eat it all the time and he thanks Sam for forcing him to try it.

Of course you don't want to be quite as persistent as Sam was in that one sales pitch. But persistence is a key ingredient to success. It may mean that you work a prospect overtime to eventually get a sale. Stick with it.

By the way, this book is high on the suggested reading list.

The one part that Sam didn't do effectively was to listen to the Cat or even ask the right questions. When talking to clients, or anybody for that matter, you "sell" by asking questions and then listening. Ask probing open-ended questions that begin with *what, why, how, where,* and *who*. Many professionals use the same techniques in their work. An attorney calls this process the "discovery." A doctor calls it a "diagnosis." And when you boil it down, it means that it is impossible to find a solution to someone's problems if you don't know what the problems are first. And you can't find the problems unless you ask a lot of questions and listen carefully to the answers.

If Sam-I-Am was aware of this, he probably would have changed his choice closes to probing informational questions. "Tell me please what you dislike, before I go and take a hike." At least now Sam-I-Am might begin to find out what the problem is.

Some people in sales refer to this as finding the "pain." You probe, using open-ended questions, to find out the pain. Once you know what a client's pain is, and he or she also knows what the pain is, it is much easier to work toward a solution.

This means you not only have to ask questions, but you have to ask the right kind of questions. As mentioned, open-ended questions usually begin with *who, what, why, where,* and *how*. They ask for information. You continue the probing by urging the client to give you additional information about a subject. You do this by simply asking him to continue:

"That's interesting, tell me more."

"Why do you say that?"

"I see. Go on."

"Why is that important to you?"

Your facial expressions need to be appropriate as well. Show concern. Make eye contact. Nod in agreement or disbelief, as the situation dictates. When the client asks you a question, first answer it briefly, then follow up with one of your own. This is usually when the client is looking for emotional support. He might say something like, "Do you think that's fair?" To which you respond with "What do you think?" or "How fair do you think it is?"

Staying in Control With the Echo

One way to stay in control of the conversation and, at the same time, gain much valuable information is to use a technique called the "echo." We first learned this from Bill Bishop a number of years ago and it really works great. The idea originally came from psychotherapists. If you have ever been to one, you may have noticed that they always answer a question with a question.

"Well, Doc, do you think I'm crazy?"

"Well, Jeff, do *you* think you're crazy?"

This always drove me up a wall, which is probably good for repeat business. At any rate, this keeps them in control, and more importantly they want you to come up with your own solution. If it is your idea, you are more likely to buy into it.

The same applies in sales. Here is how the echo works. You take the last few words of your prospect's comments and echo it back as a question. So it may sound something like this:

"The problem I have is that I'm not sure how this applies to our situation."

"Your situation?"

"Yeah, you know with the merger going on."

"The merger?"

"Yeah. It's a real problem. This company from overseas is making an offer on the company and we really don't know where we stand."

"Where you stand?"

"Well, they may want to cut some of the personnel to reduce overhead."

This is a great way to extract information without having to do too much thinking. It gives you the opportunity to figure out the best way to handle the prospect.

When Bill first told me this technique, I was excited. I was flying back to Columbus, Ohio, from Orlando, and I thought it might be a good time to try it out on Jodi, the love of my life. She was picking me up at the airport. She always complained that I did not pay enough attention to her (that was pretty much on target), so I thought this might just help turn things around. I get in the car. Instead of staring off into space as I usually did when I returned from a trip, I turned to her and led off with a question about the kindergarten class she teaches. "How were the kids today?"

She was excited. I am paying attention to her and her eyes light up. "Oh, the kids were fine but the assistant superintendent brought some parents into my room."

"*Your* room?"

"Yeah. Apparently he wanted to show them a child-centered classroom."

"Child-centered?"

"Yeah. Most classrooms are pretty dull. But I have displays everywhere. It really stimulates the children and they enjoy learning more."

"Learning more?"

"Really. Most of my kids often end the year reading and writing because I use the 'whole language' approach, which incorporates big books and inventive spelling techniques. The kids really learn faster."

"Faster?"

"I use a lot of children's literature and then create different activities that allow the kids to experience the ideas. I've attended a bunch of conferences on it the past few years."

I kept her going for thirty-five minutes all the way home from the airport. I did not say more than twenty-five words. I knew everything about her life and she very little about mine... which was pretty much what I wanted. My echo technique worked. She thought I was the most warm, sensitive, caring individual in the world. It worked so well that a few years later we were married. Now, that's a sale.

As you begin to use it you will get a little more comfortable with it. Be warned, however, that if you echo too much, some people start to catch on. After about five or six echoes they will look at you with a funny expression on their faces and say, "What's wrong with you, are you an echo?"

So you might want to alternate it a little using a few other approaches. One that works very much the same way is simply "Oh?" No matter what the prospect says, you respond with "Oh?" and they come back with more details. You can use echoes and an oh, echoes and an oh. You'll keep them going for hours if you want to.

How Solving Their Problems Clinches the Commitment

People do not buy products and services, but rather, they buy solutions to problems. It should not be that way. As a professional you want to help fill your clients' needs. You see, people do not buy goods and services; they buy solutions to problems. You must function as a problem solver to your clients. Therefore, when they have objections, they put up barriers that you must begin to break down so that you can help them solve their problems.

Heidi Knobonitch is the manager of Special Projects for Sony Music Canada, Inc. (formerly CBS Records). It's her job to approach companies about using tapes, records, and CDs for promotional programs or gifts. It takes a very creative approach when selling packaged music. In fact, she must understand a client's problem first. Then, using her product, she provides a creative solution to that problem.

Heidi did this *twice* with the Royal Bank of Canada. The bank's first goal was to sell more Visa cards. Their problem was motivating their tellers to sell the card service. Heidi suggested a contest. Every time tellers signed someone new for a Visa card, they got their names put in a drum at their branch. The more they signed, the more chances they got. Once a week names were drawn for free music tapes. The tapes that were given away as prizes were in-stock tapes from the CBS Records catalog.

According to Heidi, the Royal Bank sold "g'zillion" Visa cards, which is music business talk for a big success. For Heidi it was the twenty thousand tapes sold as prizes that made this solution very profitable for her and her client.

The follow-up promotion also involved an employee incentive program using music cassettes. The Royal Bank of Canada wanted to introduce a new financial product to their customers. The usual course of action is to print a fancy full-color brochure to give to customers. To be really successful they knew they needed their tellers to promote the new product. Heidi to the rescue once again.

She proposed that each teller receive a special audio music cassette tape with popular selections from their artists. This is not an item that an employee would toss. Then the tape box insert was printed with extra panels explaining to the teller about the product offered by the bank.

The idea worked so well that they've used it two more times to introduce new products. Heidi has a satisfied client using her products to solve their problems.

CHAPTER 9

How to Make an Effective First Contact and Avoid Wasting Your Time

Before you can use your problem-solving and question-asking techniques, you have to get an appointment with a potential client. The most direct way to find prospective clients is by telephone. It is perhaps the most effective marketing tool you have at your disposal. There are many advantages for telephone marketing. They include:

1. No risk. In most other forms of marketing you pay whether the prospect sees or reads your ad. In telephone marketing, by contrast, you only pay when you make contact. Even for out-of-town clients long-distance services are very affordable.

2. No waste. Like direct mail, telephone marketing allows you to target in on a very specific group. No other form of advertising can target as specifically as these two.

3. Interactive. Telephone marketing is the only

form of advertising that allows you to have a conversation with your prospect. The only other way to do this is to make a personal call. It allows you to qualify, field objections, and probe for needs and problems of a prospective client.

4. Saves time and money. When you compare telephone marketing to personal visits, you'll find that telephone marketing saves you substantially. You can handle five to ten times as much when you use the phone instead of personal visits.

5. Integrates easily with other marketing methods. You can use almost any other form of advertising and marketing in conjunction with your telephone. The phone can even be used for setting up qualified appointments so when you do make personal visits you get the most out of your effort.

6. Flexibility. You can be as aggressive or as subtle as you like using telephone marketing. The ways you adapt the telephone to your marketing program dictate the degree of delicacy you use.

BIG PROBLEMS WITH TELEPHONE MARKETING

1. Call reluctance. The number one problem with telephone marketing is that most people hate making marketing calls. Call reluctance is the biggest problem keeping most people from getting the clients they want.

2. Reduces contact intensity. When using the telephone instead of an in-person call, you are at a disadvantage. The in-person call makes more impact. You are in much greater control of the situation.

3. Saturation. There is a dramatic increase in telemarketing. Telemarketing clutter makes it more difficult for someone using the phone to get through to prospects.

THIS IS NOT "TELEMARKETING"

The telephone marketing approach suggested here is not to be confused with traditional telemarketing. Telemarketing reminds us of long-winded callers reading from scripts. They are often ill trained and know little about what they're selling. They have little regard for their prospects and are often rude, obnoxious, and unempathetic.

By contrast, the approach you'll use is a sophisticated and effective way to reach potential clients. When done properly, you'll come off as a professional showing concern for the prospective client. You'll get rejection. There's no way around that. But you'll also get results if you do it right and do it often.

For years in our company we relied solely on publicity and referral to get clients. It worked fine, but there were many peaks and valleys in our sales. We had little control over the timing and quality of the clients we got. In mid-1986 we started using a consistent, organized telephone marketing approach and have steadily built up the number of clients and the quality of clients. It's simple but it's not easy. You have to make a commitment to telephone calls weekly if it is to work.

Very little of this approach is original. Because of our own needs, we read almost every book and listened to every tape on the subject. People like Bill Bishop and George Walther helped us. Then we took the tons of material and began to distill and fine-tune. We modified, adapted, and simplified. This use of the telephone is based on our own experience. We know these ideas work. They work in our company and they work for our clients. It's up to you to apply this information and adapt it specifically to work for you.

Making the First Call

The telephone prospecting process that is described here assumes the lowest common denominator. That is, let's assume that you know very little about the lead and your phone call is your first contact. Once you understand and master this approach, the process is much easier for any situation where you've already had some previous contact with that person.

It's always more effective if you know the name of the person you want to call. If you don't, first conduct a "research call." Call the receptionist and ask for the name of the person responsible for buying what you're selling. There's usually very little resistance. If asked, just say that you need to send the president some information and need to know the proper spelling of his or her name. Once you know the name of that prospect, you are ready to make contact.

Getting Past the Gatekeeper

All the sales techniques are worthless unless you get to communicate with the decision maker. Unfortunately, there is usually a buffer or filter between you and the decision maker. That person, whether you call him or her a secretary, assistant, or even a gatekeeper, has the ability to keep you from talking to the right person.

The Five Variables. There are many ways of dealing with the gatekeeper. The approach you use, and the success you have with it, oftentimes depends on many influences. These may include:

1. Your personal selling style
2. The personality of the gatekeeper

3. The specific product or service you sell
4. The organization or prospect type you sell to
5. Relationship between the gatekeeper and decision maker

Though the gatekeeper may be tough to get past, this can work to your advantage. It has often been suggested that the tougher the gatekeeper, the easier the decision maker. So, once past a tough gatekeeper, you may discover you have an easier task getting the client. The key is knowing how to work past the gatekeeper.

The gatekeeper is a potentially dangerous person to your success because he or she cannot say yes but can say no. It is their job to screen calls. If this person allowed every person who called to talk to the decision maker, very little would ever be done. So it is the gatekeeper's job to make sure that the few that do get through are important. Your objective is to impress upon the gatekeeper the importance of your call; still, make sure that you give the absolute minimum amount of information required to talk to the decision maker.

It is often difficult to describe the relationship between the decision maker, the gatekeeper, and the person making the call. While watching a Monday night football game the comparison hit us. The commentator was drawing plays on the TV screen, and many of those plays seemed to parallel the different strategies used to reach the decision maker through a gatekeeper.

Here is how it works. You are the quarterback and it is your job to get the ball to the end zone and score a goal. You have many different strategies to help you do it, and the biggest obstacle between you and the end zone is the defensive line. It is their job to keep you from reaching the end zone, and they will do anything in their power to protect their goal.

In your huddle you select a given strategy that you are going to use to get the ball past the defensive line (gatekeeper). Your options are:

1. A run up the middle
2. An end run
3. A reversal
4. A quarterback sneak
5. A bomb
6. The punt
7. A screen pass

THE RUN UP THE MIDDLE

This is your most direct approach and when done properly, usually your most effective approach. The reason for its higher rate of success is that in a "run up the middle" you have more "verbal" blockers helping you. Your offensive line helps you bob and weave your way to the goal. Remember, never sell your product or service to the "buffer" or "filter." Only sell that person on putting you through to the decision maker.

The key point to this move is that you do not want to put yourself in a vulnerable position of selling your product or service to a secretary. Since the secretary is not the decision maker, you are wasting your time and you put yourself in a position of never being able to get through.

A good screener asks you many questions to get as much information as he or she can before allowing you to talk to the boss. It is like an oral game of tennis, with you serving and the secretary returning the volley with a question.

Asking questions to control the conversation works in reverse when you are talking to the gatekeeper. You want very little information from the gatekeeper, but you do want him or her to take a specific action: putting you through to the decision maker.

By using questions, you control your conversation with the gatekeeper. You use questions differently from the way you would with your prospect. When talking with the gatekeeper, you *respond to a question* but follow up *with a command*. Then *you* use the question to confirm that your command is understood.

For example, when you ask, "Is Mr. Smith in, please?" that is a question that requires a yes or no response. When you follow it up with "May I speak to him?" you are in effect asking the secretary's permission, which again gives the secretary the opportunity to say no. Those types of questions put your gatekeeper in control of *you*.

You turn that around by giving an order, thus avoiding being in a position of asking for permission. This may be a subtle difference, but when you combine it with a firm but pleasant tone in your voice, you come across in a more authoritative manner and increase your chances of getting through.

Secretaries know that part of their job is to screen calls. The degree that screeners feel you must be screened often depends on the wishes of their decision makers. But it can also arise from the screener's own perception of his or her role. Often screeners do not feel they have done their job suitably unless they ask some questions. Some even feel that the more questions you are asked, the better they are doing their job. Therefore, the secretary often asks you questions regardless of how trivial they are. It's only after these secretaries feel that they are doing their job properly, and assuming you gave no information that causes them not to put you through to the decision maker, that you stand a chance of getting through.

Finally, never lie. If you lie to a secretary, you lose all your credibility. I know that some salespeople have used some tall tales to get through to a prospect. You are much better off when you are not lying. Yet, you can provide just the bare minimum amount of information. The less information they have, the better your chances of getting put through to the prospect.

Keeping all this in mind, here is an example of a conversation between Marc Slutsky, a seasoned marketer, and a seasoned gatekeeper:

"Mr. Smith's office."

"Did you say that this is Mr. Smith's office?"

"Yes, I did."

"Great. Who am I speaking to?"

"This is Stacy."

"Oh, Stacy, this is Marc Slutsky calling for Mr. Smith. Please put me through."

"And who are you with?"

"I'm with SMI. Please tell Mr. Smith I'm holding long-distance for him."

At this point the questions start getting a little more difficult to answer. You may not feel totally comfortable with some of these responses but they have been effective in talking to decision makers.

"Is he expecting your call?"

"I don't believe we have set up a specific time, but please let him know I am on the line."

"And what is it regarding?"

"Let Mr. Smith know that I have the answers to the marketing questions. He is supposed to be in, isn't he?"

"Does he know you?"

"You know, I don't think we have met personally, Stacy, but I do have that information for him, so please let him know I've called. Okay?"

This is an extreme case, but let's examine why Marc used the particular answers to the questions this secretary gave him.

First, when Marc called he tried to get the name of the gatekeeper, and you will notice that he used it a few times throughout the conversation. People love to hear their own names. It does help to break down some of their resistance.

Also notice that Marc gave the very minimum information in answering each of her questions. Marc did not even offer his name until she specifically asked for it. By allowing her to ask a lot of questions, she feels she did her job of screening him properly. At the same time, Marc did not put the conversation in jeopardy by giving her enough information to make a decision not to let him through.

After the first few exchanges, he always followed up with a question to regain control and to get affirmation that she understood his request to put him through. Her later questions were more difficult to answer. She was really trying to dig in and find out the purpose of his call. If Marc responded with something like "it's about advertising," "insurance," or "investments," she could easily say that her boss was not interested. To avoid that, Marc played a little word game. He told her that he had the answer to the marketing questions. That is true. No matter what question the prospect might have about marketing, Marc had the answer to it. She may have interpreted that statement as meaning that they had been working together before or that this call was in response to some previous meeting, but he did not lie.

Marc used the same approach when she asked him if her boss knew him. If he responded with "No, but I would like to talk to him about some stocks," there would be no way to get through. On the other hand, Marc responded with "You know, I don't believe we have met personally, but I do have that information for him." You can see what kind of impression it makes. Did Marc say he knew him? No, he answered the question without telling a lie.

As you can see, it is not so much what you say, but rather what you do not say. I like to refer to this communication technique, or should we say, "missed communication" technique, as "creative avoidance."

Warning: Some people who find themselves in a position that requires a degree of marketing are disturbed or even offended by this approach. It is important that despite the approach you take, you should feel comfortable with it. If you feel like you are trying to deceive gatekeepers, do not use it. On the other hand, if you find that you are not getting through enough of the times, you might give it a try to see how it works for you. After giving it a good shot for a couple of days, you can always try another approach or go back to what you were doing before.

THE END RUN

Sometimes you just cannot get past the gatekeeper, so it becomes necessary to try to run around the defensive line. Here are a couple of ways to work around the gatekeeper when it is reasonably certain you will not get through.

Some business people have direct lines. Try calling the receptionist first and asking for your prospect's extension number and you might bypass the gatekeeper altogether.

Another end run approach is to call an entirely different department than the one you want. Say, for example, you want to call Mr. Jones in Accounts Payable and cannot seem to get past the gatekeeper. Try calling someone in Shipping and ask for Mr. Jones. They will tell you that you have reached the wrong department. Ask them to transfer you directly to Mr. Jones's office. They sometimes have a corporate directory with all the extension numbers and can put you right through.

THE REVERSAL

One approach that is particularly effective at times is to call the office of someone higher up in the organization. If you are trying to reach the executive vice-president, for example, then call the chief executive officer's office. The CEO's secretary will inform you that you have reached the wrong office and usually offers to transfer you to the right party. A call transferred from the boss's office stands a little better chance of getting through.

Calling people higher up works nicely when you are not quite sure who is the best person to talk to about your product or service. Call the president and briefly explain to him or her the purpose of your phone call. Then ask for a recommendation of the best person for you to contact about this particular area. Not only will you often get to the right person more easily, you'll also make a very powerful impression by mentioning, "Mr. Kaplan, the president recommended that I call you directly." Of course if the president personally transfers the call for you, your chances of getting through are even better.

THE QUARTERBACK SNEAK

Try calling very early in the morning. Often, busy executives get to the office by 6:00 or 7:00 in the morning, long before their secretaries show up. And when their phone rings, there is a very good chance they will answer it themselves. This also might work at lunchtime, after normal working hours, and on weekends. At lunchtime, you may be fortunate to have a substitute secretary filling in for the regular one while he or she gets something to eat. The fill-in filter is usually much easier to get through.

THE BOMB

This is a desperation move to say the least; still, occasionally you have no alternative. Time is running out on the clock. Every offensive move you have made just does not seem to do the job for some reason. Now you throw the "bomb." It is sometimes called the "Hail Mary."

The bomb requires that you break an earlier rule. You have tried everything, and the only way you are even going to get a shot at the decision maker is to sell the gatekeeper on the product or service. Chances for success are small, but if it is the only move you have left, you have to give it your best shot.

There are some types of products and services, though, where it is not quite as risky. We have noticed in our own office that one of our salespeople consistently worked the bomb successfully. Perhaps the reason for his success is due in part to his personality. He also has a great phone voice: very deep, authoritative yet nonthreatening. He is a charmer yet very persistent, but not to the point of annoying a prospect or client.

Another element that may allow him to be successful with the bomb is that he is selling a unique service. Our Streetfighting consulting and speaking services are different from the usual telephone solicitation. More times than not, the gatekeeper is convinced that she should put him through to the decision maker.

Be cautious using the bomb. It is often a disaster when the prospect perceives your offering as nonessential. The same applies for oversaturated industries. Yet if all else fails, you might as well throw the bomb!

When You Bomb, Throw the Bomb. Another version

of the bomb is using direct mail or other standard approaches to sales after you have tried your teleselling approach for getting past the gatekeeper. Elene sells original art in an exclusive midwestern art gallery. One of her clients, an attorney, had recently purchased a Stobart print when he noticed another print, also by Stobart, of Georgetown. Since he knew that is where his partner went to law school, he informed Elene that if she merely made his partner aware of this print, he would buy it.

She tried often to talk to the partner, but to no avail. She wanted to set up an appointment and bring the print in for him to see. No dice. After exhausting her gatekeeper repertoire, she decided to break the rules and throw the bomb. Her bomb was to send the partner a letter and color catalog with a picture of the Georgetown print. The next day Elene had a note on her desk informing her that an attorney had called and asked to have the print delivered.

This is a unique situation where the product was so perfect for the customer that simple awareness was all that was needed to get the sale. Here it was a mailer that helped get past the gatekeeper.

THE PUNT

Just as the name suggests, there is a time to be persistent and then there is a time to say "forget it" and go on to the next prospect. It is certainly a tough call to make. There are many more prospects out there, and if you cannot get through to this one, after you have given it a good ole college try, move on.

You might want to throw that lead in your "tickler" file and give a callback in five or six months. Circumstances have a way of changing. People retire, move, get transferred, or quit. The next time you call it may be a different game entirely.

In contrast to a game of football where you score points when you get the goal, you have not scored yet. Your teleselling touchdown only permits you the opportunity of presenting your story to the prospect. That is when the real teleselling begins.

THE SCREEN PASS

This one is last because it deals with an entirely different type of gatekeeper. This is the decision *influencer.* The decision influencer, just like the standard gatekeeper, also keeps you from talking to the decision maker directly. The difference is that usually the decision maker delegates the responsibility for gathering information about the potential purchase to an assistant who thus becomes the decision influencer. The assistant then compiles the information, forms an opinion, and presents it to the decision maker.

An influencer may in fact make the final decision, and the supervisor merely signs off on it. Another scenario is that the decision maker does not choose which one he or she wants, but rather, what he or she does not want. In other words, only "veto" power is offered. At any rate, when dealing with an influencer as opposed to an actual decision maker, you must accede to a weaker position for getting the commitment. If this is the case, getting the commitment is more difficult. Not only do you have to convince the influencer of the value of your product or service, but once the influencer "buys," you also have to teach the influencer how to sell it, on your behalf, to the decision maker.

Sometimes the influencer serves as a go-between. At any rate, when you are in this type of marketing position, the influencer is your ally. Keep in mind, however, that just because the influencer wants it does not mean you are going to get the commitment. You have to provide your influencer with all the ammunition that he or she needs to convince the final decision maker that this is the right move. In effect, you hand the ball off to this person.

Once you convince the influencer of the value of your product or service, it is very important to find out how the final decision takes place. For example, we might work with a national trade association that is considering our program for its annual convention. The association's programming committee has to approve or vote for whom it wants. Committees are tough. It is very difficult to control the process because the decision is done by a group instead of an individual. The difficulty compounds itself when you do not have direct access to the committee. Instead, you have to work through an influencer who presents your case, on your behalf, to the group.

In this predicament you may find it useful to learn some things about the committee, including its size and when it meets to decide on your product or service. To help your influencer, provide him or her enough sets of your promotional materials for each member of the committee. It makes a much greater impression on a committee member to have color brochures and quality reprints of testimonial letters displayed in a professional-looking folder. The committee reviewing a dozen poor-quality photocopies of the same material stapled together is very likely to be less swayed.

It is also important to find out from your influencer what some committee members' main objections are, if possible. Sometimes they have time to review your material before the meeting. So consider contacting a few of the members for their feedback and possible objections. Then you work with your influencer on how to handle those particular objections. This is important because often the influencer is not a proficient salesperson and, of course, does not have the product knowledge that you do. So help prepare that influencer as strongly as you can.

This same approach works when the influencer is presenting to a single decision maker. Again, you have to help your influencer present the information so that you are most likely to get a favorable response.

You also may find yourself dealing with an influencer when you have already talked to the decision maker. Your call allowed you to present to the boss, but then he or she refers you to the assistant who is handling the details. If your discussion with the boss went well, especially well enough to get referred, then you are on strong ground. Seize the opportunity with the decision maker to discover all the possible roadblocks. Then, when you are working with the influencer, you can help him or her best prepare to get the commitment, provided you have an influencer who is already committed to your product or service.

The Four Steps to Get the Client to Talk to You

The most critical part of your phone call is your "opener." The opener is the first ten to twenty seconds of talking directly with your prospect. There are four steps to the opener:

Step 1. Introduction
Step 2. Benefit Statement
Step 3. New News
Step 4. Permission to Pursue

Your Introduction. Step one of your opener is to introduce yourself and the company you represent. One technique suggested for a more effective opener is repeating the prospect's name to make sure you do, in fact, have the right person on the line. Here is an example of the first line in the opener using this approach:

"Mr. McQuay?" (Wait for a response like "Yes" or "You got him.") "This is Jeff Slutsky with Streetfighter Marketing in Columbus, Ohio."

In that first sentence, Mr. McQuay heard his name. He responds to you, which immediately involves him in your conversation. This is important because you cannot see your lead over the phone. You don't know if he or she is paying attention or is busy with other things. Asking a question forces him to participate in your conversation, which is much different from having a script reader go on for ten minutes before asking the first question.

He also knows who you are, your company or organization, and from where you're calling. The reason you mention the city is that calling long-distance seems to add a sense of urgency and importance. However, if you are making a local call, you might consider a slight change. Here is an example: "This is Jeff Slutsky from Streetfighter Marketing here in Columbus." This works best when proximity is an important feature to your prospect.

Since my name or my company probably does not mean much to Mr. McQuay, my second sentence explains in a very precise and concise way the benefits of what we offer. I want to stress how we are unique. A good "benefit statement" is even more important if your company name is well known. This is because your prospect may already think he or she knows the purpose of your call and might try to cut you off before you get an opportunity to present your benefits.

Benefit Statement. Immediately after the first sentence of your opener, launch into the sentence that explains what you do and why you are unique. In this sentence you want to provide the user benefits of what you do. In my case, I would *not* say, "We conduct seminars, workshops, and consulting projects in local store marketing." That tells Mr. McQuay just enough information so he can tell us he has no interest.

Instead, you stress the unique benefits of your products and services to the prospect. For example, I might say, "We're specialists in the area of helping businesses learn how to advertise, promote, and generally increase sales without spending money."

Now, that is a benefit. Notice that I did not mention anything about seminars or consulting. Those are details. How we do it is of little consequence. The benefits or results are the key.

Your New News. The third sentence is the "new news." We have to have a special reason for the phone call that creates a sense of urgency. It could be a new product or service you are introducing or a special introductory offer. You want one more piece of news that "sweetens" the benefit to the prospect a little more. For example, sometimes I use something like, "The reason I'm calling you is we have recently developed some new programs that many of our clients tell us are getting them tremendous response."

Permission to Pursue. Now I am ready for the fourth and final sentence of my opener: asking permission to continue our discussion. Therefore, the last sentence must be a question. And since we are asking a question to get permission to do something, it is a question that must require a yes or no response.

The problem is that the natural reaction of almost anyone who gets anything related to a telephone solicitation is to say no. They want to say no. They are conditioned to say no. They are used to ill-trained script readers calling them up and boring them to death with a pitch like, "Hi. My name is Jeff. How are you doing today? We would like you to buy tickets to the circus..."

When you start, their natural reaction is to say that they have no interest. "No, thanks anyway, but no." Since most of the people you are going to talk to on the phone are already preconditioned to say no in some fashion, we have to design the closing of our opener in such a way as to get them to respond with a "no." So we want to ask a *negative question*. In responding with a "no," they actually give an affirmative answer to our question and, therefore, permission to continue with the presentation.

So my ending question might be something like, "Is there any reason why you wouldn't want to learn a little bit more about it?"

Notice that when they respond with a "no," they are giving us an affirmative answer to the question, and we can continue right on with the presentation. So when you put it all together, it sounds like this:

"Mr. McQuay?" (Then I wait for him to respond.) "This is Jeff Slutsky of Streetfighter Marketing in Columbus, Ohio. We're specialists in the area of helping businesses learn how to advertise, promote, and generally increase sales without spending a lot of money. The reason I'm calling you is that we have just developed some new programs that our clients tell us are getting them some tremendous response. Is there any reason why you wouldn't want to learn a little more about it?"

"No."

"Great, let me ask you this . . ."

And you are right in the front door. It is that simple. You can change the wording to make it more comfortable for you and, of course, you need to find just the right description of who you are and the new news you wish to present to your prospect.

Another approach you might try, depending on the type of product or service you sell, is to add another question in the middle of the opener. This works only if giving the name of your company is not a deterrent from taking your phone call and your company name is not too widely known. It goes like this: "This is Jeff Slutsky of Streetfighter Marketing. We specialize in teaching businesses how to advertise, market, and generally increase sales without spending a lot of money. We call our unique program 'Streetfighting.' Have you heard of us?" (The listener responds.) "Well, like I said, we specialize in teaching low-cost promotional programs on the local level and we have just developed some new techniques that many of our clients tell us are getting great results. Is there any reason why you wouldn't want to learn a little bit more about it?"

In this example we sneak that extra question in of "Have you heard of us?" This brings the listener into the conversation sooner. It is also a nice piece of information to know because occasionally we get a "yes." In that case we follow up with "No kidding. How do you know us?" We want to find out what they know as well as how favorable the impression is, so we know how to proceed from there.

Usually, however, the answer is no. This then gives us an opportunity to repeat and perhaps even refine or expand the benefit statement and go on as we normally do. In the example, we added that our program is done on a local level.

This approach might not be as effective if you are from American Express or AT&T, for example. Try calling up a prospect and telling them you are with American Express and "Have you heard of us?" You do not want to insult their intelligence and get off to a bad start.

Something you might want to play with is using the prospect's name two or three times in the opener. This is a technique that telemarketing expert Stan Billue, author of *Double Your Income Selling on the Phone*, suggests. He feels that people just love to hear their own names and that by mentioning it several times in the first part of your opener, you will have a better response. It works like this:

"Mr. McQuay, please."

"This is he."

"Mr. Mike McQuay?"

"Yes."

"Mr. McQuay, my name is Jeff Slutsky with Streetfighter Marketing and . . ."

Some find it a little difficult to use this, but doing it twice seems to work fine:

"Mr. McQuay?"

"Yes."

"Mr. McQuay, my name is Jeff Slutsky. . ."

So you might play with it and see what's comfortable for you.

To give you a better idea, let's look at some other examples of openers. The first we developed for a major transportation company:

"Mr. Sanborn? This is Bob Ungar with the Doberman Package Express Service here in Denver. We specialize in shipping time-sensitive packages in the same day or the next day by 8:30 A.M. We just introduced a new introductory program that allows you to save 60 percent for the next three months. Is there any reason why you wouldn't want to learn more about it?"

Notice that all four parts of the opener are there: introduction, description of the benefit, new news, and permission to pursue.

Of course, you can change the elements in the opener whenever developments come up, but be careful not to pigeonhole yourself. For example, you just opened a new market that is new news. The prospect you call may have no need for this new market, but could benefit from your service in other ways. By offering some new news that is too specific, he or she could blow you off. So in the Doberman Package Express example it might be dangerous to use a new-news sentence like, "We've just started shipping directly to Obetz and Lima, Ohio." That gives your prospect the opportunity to respond with "We never ship to those cities. Thanks anyway."

Make sure that your new news is something that cannot get you turned down. New news can be a special price reduction, provided you do not mention that it is on just a few items. It could be any development or enhancement in service.

Another client in a discount motel chain uses an appropriate opener geared for that particular business. It might sound like the following when selling by phone to get corporate accounts:

"This is Lisa Segal with Marvelous Motor Inns here in Chicago. We specialize in providing the highest quality, comfortable motel rooms at very competitive prices. Recently, we've introduced a special corporate discount program that saves you even more money. Is there any reason why you wouldn't want to learn more about it?"

I think you have the idea. Now you need to create your own opener using the four steps.

Keep in mind that the philosophy of *not* using or reading a script differs greatly from many others in the telemarketing training arena. It is fine for the untrained, but you are a professional selling quality products and services. You should be well rehearsed. The exception is your opener, which should be scripted. Practice to the point that it does not sound like you are reading from it. It should sound unrehearsed and spontaneous.

Benefit Statement Revisited. The benefit statement that you use in your phone call is also used in many other aspects of your marketing, so it's important that you spend some time to develop and refine an effective one for your situation. One of the most challenging benefit statements we had to work on was one for a life insurance company. The minute someone says he or she sells life insurance, people head for the door. Nobody wants life insurance and they certainly don't want to talk to a salesperson about it.

The challenge was to create a benefit statement that would grab a prospect's attention and avoid the turnoff associated with life insurance. The real test for such a benefit statement is to use it at a cocktail party. In a conversation, when someone asks you what you do, the benefit statement should cause them to respond with "No kidding . . . How do you do that?" In essence they're asking you to give a sales pitch about your product or service.

The key point is to figure out the end result or the benefit gained by using this person's product. One of our life insurance saleman's major areas of concentration is helping well-to-do people have a significant retirement income. So the benefit statement developed was, "We specialize in developing a plan to help people accumulate over a million dollars for retirement with only a small monthly contribution." Nowhere did you hear the term "life insurance." It's irrelevant at this point. Clients are more interested in the end result. How they get there is detail stuff.

In the first chapter, you learned to identify and exploit your unique niche. You now want to incorporate your unique niche into your benefit statement. Ask yourself what you do that clients will find very valuable. How can you phrase it so that, when asked, most people will respond with "No kidding. How do you do that?"

For example, if you merely said that you're an accountant or a CPA, that might be of some interest. On the other hand, if you said, "I specialize in helping people dramatically reduce their tax bill," that would get most people's attention. The fact that you're a CPA will come up later in the conversation. If you stress CPA, then you're automatically lumped in with all the other CPAs.

A stockbroker might say, "I specialize in uncovering undervalued companies with strong long-term potential for people who want to maximize their investment profits."

The branch manager of a local bank might say, "I specialize in helping businesses handle just about all their finance needs, including establishing lines of credit and cash-flow management." He sells loans, CDs, and checking accounts but that's irrelevant. What's important is the result, the benefit of using this banker's services.

The Five Tests for Qualifying Your Prospect

Now that you are in the front door—and this, perhaps, is the most difficult part of your telephone selling effort—your job is just beginning. Now that you have permission to continue with the prospect, your objective is to decide whether you want to do business with this prospect. In other words, you need to qualify your prospect to see if there is the potential for a sale.

To qualify your prospect, you need to ask a lot of questions to find out some important information. But what information do you need to know to qualify this prospect? In any business there are many "qualifiers" that determine if you have the potential for getting a sale. You will find that there are often five "qualifiers" or tests your prospect needs to pass before you make a commitment to pursue the sale. Of course, every type of business is different and you may want to modify the list to best suit your particular needs. Use these five qualifiers as your starting point:

1. Want
2. Need

3. Decision maker
4. Decision mode
5. Budget/money

Want. The prospect has to want the benefit of what your product or service has to offer. If he or she does not want it, it is very hard to get a sale. Do not waste your time unless he or she wants it.

If you disqualify a prospect based on want, you need to be sure that you are not tossing out a potentially good lead. We had a painful experience with this in our own company. Our sales force was selling our consulting and speaking services over the phone. One of our tellsellers was qualifying his leads on the question of "want" using a couple of questions similar to these:

"If there was a program that allowed you to increase your sales without spending a lot of money doing so, would you like to see that program implemented in your organization?"

"Do you ever use professional speakers or trainers in your organization?"

These two particular questions are designed to get a "yes" or a "no." If we get a "no" to the first question, it means they do not want the benefits of what we have and there is no potential for doing business. A "no" to the second question means there is a problem with the way in which our services are provided to the client. We know, however, that most people we call really want the *benefit* of our program, so in a way we are asking a loaded question. Yet occasionally this type of question does flush out those who at least perceive they do not want what we have to offer.

We noticed that we were getting an unanticipated response that was hard to deal with. Of the small percentage of people who would be disqualified based on want, we did follow up a little by asking why. We found out that usually the reason they did not want us was they only used "in-house" trainers and seminar leaders. This response threw us for a loop. We could not figure out how to get around this objection.

It is hard to deal with a policy that requires using in-house trainers. It automatically takes us out of the running. Yet we wanted to work on this roadblock because we knew there had to be a way of getting around it. We called back some of our disqualified leads. This time we probed a little more to find why they only used in-house trainers and refused to use outside speakers. We discovered that they felt only someone deeply involved with their company could adequately address their particular problems. Moreover, they did not want to share proprietary information with just anybody, lest it should fall into the wrong hands. So, to keep control, they used only in-house trainers.

Oddly enough, what they were telling us was that they only work with people on an in-depth, long-term basis. That is exactly what we wanted! Once we discovered this piece of valuable information, we went to work on a follow-up response to that "no." The stumbling block was "in-house." We interpreted this to mean a full-time employee of the company and sometimes that's probably what the prospect meant too. Yet when you take the term "in-house" and expand on it, there still might be a way to work with the company. So we came up with this response: "What do we have to do to become one of your in-house trainers?"

That did the trick! By responding with that question, the prospect would explain to us exactly the type of relationship he wanted in order to consider using our services. We got more out of the conversation than we bargained for. The funny thing is that the response was so simple. It worked like a charm. We got to the point of not only qualifying them on "want" but getting additional information. As a result, we were in a stronger position to solve the prospect's problems and close the sale later.

Need. This is very much related to "want" but it is different. "Want" is a perceived desire. "Need" deals more with reality of a prospect's situation. The prospect may want what you have to offer, but not need it because of any number of reasons. The company may have already hired a competitor. Perhaps they have other priorities that they wish to take care of first, though they would like to have it. Note that we are talking in terms of the "benefits" of your product or service rather than the features.

In selling an intangible like life insurance, for example, you could ask the prospect, "Do you need life insurance?" While this question deals with the prospect's need, it is not a good question. You are not likely to get a truly accurate response with that question. The prospect may already have some coverage and was not considering more. Still, the response would be much different if you asked an entirely different question that zeroed in on the "benefit." For example, "Is it important for you to know that should something tragic happen to you, your family would not be forced into poverty?"

Granted, an extreme example, but one that does illustrate how benefits are what your prospects want and need. Painting these kinds of word pictures in the minds of your clients helps you convey to the prospect the real value of what you are offering.

If a stockbroker asks a prospect if he or she is interested in making investments or needs a stockbroker, the response is likely to be negative. The prospect may already have a stockbroker or financial planner. Yet if you were to ask if he or she wanted an investment opportunity that allowed for substantial growth, return on investment with minimal risk, you might find out that he or she wants and needs your services. It is all how you phrase the question.

The phrasing of these questions is so important that Bill Bishop, author and producer of the *Million Dollar Presentation* and *Prime Prospects Unlimited*,[28] tells the story of the young monk to illustrate this exact point. A young monk joined the monastery and wanted to ask the abbot for permission to smoke his pipe. He approached the abbot and asked, "Can I have permission to smoke my pipe when I pray?"

The abbot responded negatively to the request and the young monk accepted his decision without question. When he ventured out into the courtyard, he noticed an older monk smoking a pipe. Naturally, he wondered how this monk had been able to get permission. Curious, the younger monk approached him and explained that he had asked the abbot if he could smoke his pipe when he prayed and was turned down.

The older monk took a long puff of his pipe and responded, "Well, my brother, when I approached the abbot, I asked him an entirely different question. I asked if it was appropriate to pray while smoking my pipe. He informed me that anytime was appropriate for prayer!"

Decision Maker. The third qualifier is to find out if you are talking to the decision maker. If you are not, you are wasting your time. If the decision is made by more than one person, then it is vital that you talk to all the decision makers simultaneously. Without talking to the

---

[28]Bill Bishop, Bill Bishop & Associates, 834 Gran Paseo Dr., Orlando, FL, 32825. (407) 281-1395. Programs available in audiocassette and videotapes only.

decision maker, you cannot get a "yes" and, therefore, you are wasting your time.

Sometimes, you may find that you are forced to deal with a decision influencer. For example, when a client is considering our program, the final decision is often made by a board of directors. Usually the association's convention coordinator does not let me talk to the board members directly. So I have to sell our program through the coordinator, who takes it to the board. I know it is a much weaker sale because I cannot deal directly with the decision makers.

Decision Mode. The fourth qualifier is decision mode. Can your prospect make a decision within a certain time? If you are selling copy or fax machines and your prospect just bought one a year ago, you know that he or she probably will not be in a decision-making mode for at least another year unless the company is planning an expansion or is not happy with its current equipment. Knowing your prospect's buying cycle is very important.

Budget. The fifth qualifier is money. Is your prospect willing to spend the money for what you are selling? Now, do not confuse willingness to spend the money with affordability. When someone tells you he cannot afford it, that is an opinion, not necessarily a statement of fact. The prospect is telling you that you have not convinced him enough to justify the expenditure.

You have to be careful with this one because often prospects will tell you that they can only spend a certain amount of money. Yet if you offer them such a terrific opportunity or they understand the value of what you have to offer them, price is not a problem. But you still have a way to go before you reach the close. And just as important, you learn how to reinforce your qualifying call with the proper mail follow-up.

So what kind of questions do you ask to decide if he or she is qualified? Here are some suggestions.

How to Find the Real Decision Maker

Let's start with the decision maker. This one is easy because it is the same question for any business. You do not want to ask, "Are you the decision maker?" because this challenges their egos too much and you are likely to get a "yes" when, in fact, they are not.

The question I like to use is, "With whom else would you want to consult before you make your final decision?"

See how nonthreatening this is? Once someone tells you he is the decision maker and would not have to consult anyone else, often he is not. So I like to double-check it with a follow-up question: "That's great. So you're the head person in charge. Wonderful. Let me ask you this. Once you make your decision, whose name actually appears on the contract?"

I know it sounds tough, but let me tell you, it does flush out a lot of gofers from the real decision makers.

Discovering Needs and Wants

To find out if the prospect needs and wants what you have, you must ask some open-ended questions. I like to start out with something that immediately gets the prospect to do the talking.

Questions you might ask to discover wants and needs would be the ones that tell you whether they are using your type of product or service now or have used it in the past. For life insurance you might ask, "What kind of coverage do you currently have?" The same holds true for investment: "What kind of investments are you currently involved in?"

This will start to open some doors. When you start to get this type of information, probe a little deeper to find out why they have what they have. Then find out what they like most about what they have now and what they like least. To do this, ask your questions diplomatically; because, when trying to find out what they dislike about their present product or service, you do not want to offend them by implying that they made a bad decision.

So, to discover want and need, you might use the following series of questions. Let's take investments as an example, with Marc representing an up-and-coming young stockbroker, qualifying a lead whom we'll call Mr. Nelson.

"Mr. Nelson, what kinds of investments are you currently involved in? Stocks, bonds, CDs?"

"Well, mostly CDs and some mutual funds."

"I see. What is it about CDs and mutual funds that you like?"

"With the CDs there's very little risk, so I do not have to worry about the bottom falling out. But I do like to get a little more return so I'll buy into a solid mutual fund occasionally. I like them because I don't have to watch the stocks every day. Watching them go up and down drives me up a wall and my doctor wants me to watch my blood pressure... you know what I mean?"

"I heard that. So if I understand you correctly, you want investments that are primarily safe, yet give a decent return; but you like to spice up an investment from time to time with something just a little more aggressive, as long as you do not have to deal with it on a day-to-day basis. Is that a fair assessment?"

"Yep."

"Mr. Nelson, in the past when you have made investments, other than that particular investment not performing as well as you liked, is there anything about dealing with it that you thought could have been handled better?"

"Come to think of it, there was a broker I was using before the one I got now who would never return my phone calls. I thought that was very unprofessional and it annoyed me a lot. You know?"

"I understand. It sounds like your broker now is doing a good job for you."

"He is. Always returns my calls. Doesn't bother me too much with stuff I'm not interested in."

"I see. Let me ask you this. If there were one thing that he is doing now that you could change, what would it be?"

"Well, he is almost too passive. I mean, I'll know about some new investments that are out before he does, and I'm usually the one who has to suggest ideas to him."

"That makes sense. Mr. Nelson...let me ask you this. I know you're working with this broker now, and it sounds like he is doing a pretty good job for you, but if I could provide you with some investment opportunities that could potentially boost your return significantly, yet had only moderate risk and was something that you wouldn't have to worry about day to day, would you consider it for part of your portfolio?"

"I don't see why not."

"Super. Let me ask you just a few more questions..."

You see, the open-ended questions that Marc asked the prospect opened up a special need and a want, even though the prospect already had someone providing him a similar service. You will notice that it was only after the prospect told Marc what he wanted and what he did not want that Marc knew which way to guide the prospect.

He found his "hot buttons." Then he asked a "trial clos-ing" question just to see how serious the prospect was: "If I could do this . . . would you do this?"

So the questions involve: What have you done? What are you doing? Why are you doing it? What do you like about what you are doing? If you could change anything about the way you're doing it, what would it be? Notice, you don't ask what they do *not* like. You'll not get the response you want.

It's also very important that you do not cut down your competitor. It will be perceived as unprofessional. Stress your benefits.

Secondary Supplier. If you're having trouble break-ing into a client that seems very happy with his or her current arrangement, try the "secondary supplier" ap-proach. Craig Adler, of German Village Travel, uses this successfully.

Suggest to the client that you understand he or she is happy. However, the best business people always have a backup supplier just in case. Every once in a while there might be an emergency or a backlog. Just use us once in a while so we can keep you on our books and when you need us, we'll be there for you.

This approach usually gives little resistance. It's a foot in the door. Then when their primary supplier screws up, you get the business.

Uncovering the Real Budget

Now let's look at qualifying budget. This qualifier is fairly straightforward. You first figure out, as best you can, in which price level your prospect falls. Then you say something like, "Our clients usually fall into three catego-ries. Those that want to invest just a few thousand dollars a year, usually into their IRAs, then the middle ground of five thousand to fifteen thousand, and of course the more aggressive investors who will invest twenty thousand or more. In which of these categories do you see yourself?"

The middle category is the one where you anticipate your prospect, but occasionally you might be surprised. Once they pick a category, they have told you that they have the money to do it, provided the opportunity warrants the investment. Budget is qualified.

When you're asked about your fees, give a straightforward answer without delay. Often when people are asked about fees, they feel uncomfortable and respond almost apologetically. Sound firm but not arrogant. "Our fee for that service is three thousand. Is that in your budget?" Always follow up a price with the question "Is that in your budget?" or "Is that in the ballpark?" You must get their response to the fee or price you've just mentioned. If there is fee or price resistance, find out now so you can deal with it.

Find out How Long Before You Get the Check

Now you need to qualify on decision mode. You ask, "If there was an investment that you felt was exactly what you wanted, is there any reason you couldn't take advantage of it right away?"

Here you are trying to find out if there is anything that could keep you from getting a decision now. Perhaps your prospect has all his or her money tied up into two-year CDs and cannot get it out for another year and a half. That would disqualify your prospect for now, but of course you would put that prospect in your tickler file to contact perhaps in a year or so.

With these questions answered, you should now have

a good feeling about your prospect. You know he or she wants and needs your product or service. The person you are talking to can make a decision, and he or she has the money and the capacity to spend it now. All the elements are in place. Congratulations, you got yourself a qualified prospect.

But do not be in a hurry to pat yourself on the back. Qualifying your prospect is very important, but you are far from getting a sale.

CHAPTER 10

How to Set up Appointments That Set up Commitments

Now that your prospect is qualified, you have just begun the selling process. The next phase is critical whether you want to use the phone to set up an in-person appointment or you want to use the phone for the entire selling process. The purpose of the second contact, whether by phone or in person, is to requalify, then start probing in greater detail to find out the real and perceived needs of your prospect.

The Four Objectives of the Initial Contact

You have four objectives before you are done with this first contact. The first is to qualify your prospect. You learned this is the preceding chapter. The second is to set up a specific time for your next contact. The third is to prepare your prospect to receive your first follow-up mailer if contact is by phone. And your last objective is to get referrals.

As mentioned before, it makes no difference if you are going to meet your prospect in person or continue to use the telephone for your marketing effort. You still set up a specific time for your next meeting. So if your next meeting happens to be over the phone, you still set up the appointment so you have a better chance of connecting with your prospect and thus avoid what George Walther refers to as "telephone tag."

The follow-up mailing is important and does a couple of things for you, but first you have to get your prospect to read it. Remember, most so-called junk mail gets tossed out. But just as you get a specific commitment from your prospect to meet with you for the second time, you also get a specific commitment from your prospect to look for and read your follow-up mailer.

Setting up a Qualified Appointment

First, let's set up the appointment. Setting up the appointment is somewhat the same for either an in-person visit or your next telephone meeting.

Once you qualify and *you have* determined that you want to do business with this prospect, you make a suggestion that you get together again so you can discuss it in more detail. You might use something like this:

"Well, Mr. McQuay, it sounds like we might have what you're looking for. What I'd like to do first is send you some information to give you a better idea of who we are and how we might help you. Then, after you have had time to review it, we'll get together again, over the phone, so I can get your feedback to it. Would that be okay?"

Getting Commitment to Review Your Mailer. At this point you want for him to say yes to the question of "Okay?" Now you have his commitment to review the mailer as well as his commitment to set up an appointment to talk again. Also notice that nonthreatening terms are being used. The presentation is softened greatly by using "might" a few times. If you come on too strong at this point, it could turn off your prospect. Also notice that I ask for his *feedback* to the information. Again, this is very nonthreatening. I'm not asking for a decision that puts your prospect on edge. Feedback is asking for advice or guidance.

Getting the Next Appointment. Now you set up the appointment. You do this by talking out loud to your prospect. It would sound something like this:

"Let's see, Mr. McQuay. I can get our information kit out today, which means you'll probably get it Wednesday or Thursday. You'll want a couple of days to review the materials, which puts us at next Tuesday... a week from tomorrow. So I'll get back to you a week from Wednesday. Is that a good day for you?"

If it is a good day, the next step is to set up a specific time for the phone call. If it is a bad day, then you obviously find a good day first. So you would continue:

"What's a good time when you could give me fifteen to twenty minutes uninterrupted?"

Whatever time your prospect suggests, consider making the appointment for a little after it, usually at a slightly odd time. For example, if your prospect says that 10:00 A.M. is a good time, you think out loud and say, "Ooohhh, I'm busy at ten but, I have ten after ten open, is that close enough for you?"

By using odd times like ten, twenty, forty, or fifty minutes after the hour, you give the impression to your prospect that you are very busy, which you are. They get a sense that your time is very valuable, which it is. It also looks peculiar in their appointment book or calendar, which keeps drawing attention to you. George Walther suggests that you might even talk the prospect through the process of writing the appointment down to further reinforce it. That would sound like:

"Do you have your appointment book handy there? Good, do me a favor and write me down for ten-ten on the twenty-sixth, I'll do the same on my end. Okay?"

Finally I close the conversation by reinforcing the appointment time and the arrival of my mailer. It sounds like this:

"Great. I've got you down for ten-ten A.M. next Thursday the twenty-sixth. Now, I'll send out the information you requested today. You'll recognize it because it'll be in a large nine-by-twelve black envelope with our white mailing label with a very bright red 'Streetfighter' printed on it. That should get your attention, you think? And by the way, if for some reason you need to change our meeting, please give me a call so I could free up that time. Okay?

"Super. Thanks a lot, Mr. McQuay, and I'll be looking forward to talking to you on the twenty-sixth...Oh, by the way, who else do you know who could benefit from a program that helps businesses advertise, promote, and increase sales without spending a lot of money? Perhaps another franchisee, supplier, or friend?

"And why do you recommend them?

"When I call, is there any reason why I shouldn't mention your name?

"Great. And who else do you know that...

"I really appreciate these referrals and I promise I'll contact them right away. And I'll be looking forward to chatting with you on the twenty-sixth. Thanks again. Bye."

Notice that the word "appointment" is not used with the prospect when referring to the meeting. "Appointment" is a negative word. Rather, the word "meeting" is used. Very positive. The word "meeting" is even used to describe the next telephone call. This adds a great deal more importance to future conversations.

Also notice how he has committed to looking for the mail piece. It is no longer a piece of junk mail because he is specifically looking for it. Unlike junk mail, which gets a readership of maybe 2 to 3 percent, with this approach you are likely to get a readership that reaches toward 100 percent.

Mailing a Follow-up With Impact

The purpose of your follow-up mailer, or "info kit," is to reinforce the benefits you discussed in your conversation. It also helps build additional credibility for your product or service, your company, and finally for you—in that order. Finally you want to remind your prospect of your upcoming meeting.

You don't want to use your literature to "sell" your product or service. Don't give your prospect any "nuts and bolts" information about your program . . . only the benefits. You see, once your prospect has enough information, especially pricing information, he or she can make a decision; and the only decision your prospect can make without you there to guide them is "no." You want to save all your technical information and prices for the phone call, so you can control the conversation.

We call it an info kit because it contains several elements. For maximum flexibility, the information is provided in a simple folder. These folders can be custommade or very simple, depending on your budget. We use a plain two-pocket folder. Our logo is in the lower right-hand corner in red foil. The right pocket is die-cut for a business card. There is no address, phone, or other information anywhere on the folder.

Then we customize the info kit to meet the needs of the specific client. Our info kits usually contain, but are not limited to, the following four elements:

1. Cover letter
2. Testimonial letters
3. Publicity reprints
4. Generic brochure

COVER LETTER

The first element of your info kit is the cover letter. This is also the most important. It must be a customized letter, written specifically to your prospect. Don't use a preprinted form letter. However, it is perfectly acceptable to use a word-processed letter with the client's name and the client's company name mentioned throughout.

The cover letter is a slight variant of the sales letter discussed in the chapter on direct mail. The difference is that the cover letter is reinforcing a previous conversation.

Your first sentence is important because it is your headline. It should jump out and capture your prospect's interest so much that he or she wants to read the rest of the letter. Use the word "you" a lot in your letter and stress those benefits.

On the facing page is a letter that I use when selling my consulting and speaking services. I've used Segal's Hot Dogs, a mythical chain of hot-dog stands in and around the Chicago area, as the pretend client.

[Date]

Ms. Lisa Segal
President & CEO
Segal's Hot Dogs, Inc.
166 Wacker Dr.
Chicago, IL 60606

Dear Lisa:

It was a pleasure talking with you today about how each of your Segal's Hog Dogs locations can increase sales greatly on a shoestring budget using our effective Streetfighting local store marketing program.

As you know, our Streetfighting local store marketing program has received some national attention from publications like *The Wall Street Journal, USA Today,* and *Inc. Magazine* to name a few. This unique program would be developed specifically for your locations.

You'll find that our Streetfighting program is a welcome addition to your Segal's Hot Dogs marketing efforts, and each of your locations can implement these very effective, easy-to-do sales-building programs.

I have enclosed some background material for you that gives you a close view of how our program benefits your operation. I look forward to talking with you Thursday, November 26, at 10:10 in the morning.

Best wishes,

Jeff Slutsky
President

P.S. John Smith, of ABC Company, writes, "Your program was very well done and extremely useful."

Notice that the letter gives Ms. Segal absolutely no nuts-and-bolts information, just benefits, credibility, and reinforcement. I want to bring this prospect along slowly so that we begin to build rapport and trust. The more individual contact we have, either by phone, in person, fax, or through the mail, the more she feels she really knows me; so I want both frequency and quality of contacts.

The next critical element of your cover letter is the P.S. It is usually the first thing people read. As soon as they open the letter, they first look for the signature to see who it is from, and then they notice the P.S. So you always want to have a post script in your sales letter. Use one that grabs the reader's attention and causes enough interest to get him or her to go back and read the rest of your letter.

Also notice that throughout the letter the word "you" or "your" is used eleven times. Everybody wants to know what is in it for them. Don't talk in terms of "I do this" or "we do that" but rather in terms of "you get this" or "you are provided with that."

Just as powerful is mentioning the client's name several times in the letter. This grabs the reader's attention and is very easy to do on any word processor.

BROCHURE

Other items in your info kit can be any kind of generic promotional material you have around the office. For example, we always enclose our generic brochure, but before we do, we use different color highlighters on key phrases, handwritten notes in the margin directed at the reader, and Post-it notes. This shows that you have had personal involvement in the piece. By taking your slick, professionally produced brochure and intentionally making it ugly, you'll get much more attention from your reader.

If you're thinking about creating a brochure, I'd think

it through very carefully. They can be very costly. The alternative is to use single sheets that can be inserted into your folder. When one of the sheets promoting a certain service becomes outdated, it's very easy and less expensive to replace than redoing your entire brochure.

HOW TO GET GLOWING TESTIMONIALS FROM CLIENTS

Other items might include a couple of testimonial letters of recommendation from satisfied clients. This is perhaps the only item you'll need to go outside your office to get. You'll also use more of them later in the selling process, but a couple of strong ones at this point are helpful.

The best time to get such a letter is right after you've completed some work for a client. If the client is clearly very happy with you, make your suggestion: "You know, I'm very happy that we were able to work with you. It would really be helpful if you could send me a letter, on your letterhead, with a few of those thoughts. Would that be okay?" Often a satisfied client is more than happy to provide you such a letter. He or she usually feels honored that you've asked.

Most clients will agree to write you a letter, but in reality only some do. It's not a high priority for them. If you don't get a letter in a reasonable time, you might try calling back. Often they're very apologetic but they've been busy, etc. So, based on the previous conversation, you offer to write the letter for them. Then they can make changes, if necessary, and have it typed on their letterhead.

It makes it much easier on them, and with you controlling the text of the letter, you're more likely to get a letter with a little extra potency. No one can write a testimonial for you, like you.

To make it even easier on the client, you can suggest that he or she send a few pieces of stationery over to you. Then you have your secretary type up the letter. Send it back to the client for approval and signature. Then have it mailed back to you in a self-addressed stamped envelope. The easier you make it, the more likely you are to get the letter. And you get one that really "sells."

To start getting your testimonial letters, go back to your past clients. Choose clients with whom you have a good rapport. Look at your client list and mark off the ones you feel comfortable contacting. Now contact them.

Testimonial letters need to become an ongoing part of your marketing effort. The more you collect, the more ammunition you have for your marketing efforts. It's good to have letters with older and newer dates. This shows consistency over time. A variety of letters, dealing with different problems, are helpful too. This allows you to select the most appropriate letters when contacting a potential client.

There is another way you can use the testimonial. When you're talking to a prospective client, you can give him some of your past satisfied clients as references. Obviously you want to have permission from that satisfied client to use his name and to have a prospect call him about you. This is also very powerful.

Excerpts and quotes are effective brochure copy. Again, you want to have permission to use quotes from your clients. Usually they're pleased to do it because it's extra exposure for them. Providing a contact name and company responsible for the quote is more powerful than anonymous credit. It's worth the extra trouble of getting their permission. And if for some reason they don't want their name or company mentioned, it's good that you find out now. It's not worth jeopardizing the client relationship.

To make more impact with your testimonial letters, and if your budget allows, consider reprinting them to resemble the originals. That is, reproduce the letters on letterhead quality paper first. This does not add much to the cost but will be very impressive in your info kit. Your quick printer usually has a number of different letterhead papers in stock. Use different ones.

To make even more impact and as the budget allows, consider printing the letters in colors. Your printer can create it to look very similar to the client's original. This works exceptionally well when the client's logo is recognizable. We did this for some of our clients, including Domino's Pizza, American Express, AT&T, Greyhound, Firestone, McDonald's, and National Car Rental.

You don't have to match the paper exactly. We find out what our printer has in stock and wants to get rid of. They usually carry a variety of letterhead quality papers and there is usually some they're stuck with and will make a deal on. When you print these, have the printer print all the ones using the same colors at the same time. It saves you a big setup fee. Or if you have a good relationship with your printer, have him or her contact you when they have a certain color on the press. They get a two-color run but don't have to set the press up specifically for you.

Another little trick is to have them print the signature in blue if there is blue in the logo. It really makes your letters look original. The cost of these two- and three-color runs is obviously much more, anywhere from twelve to twenty cents per piece in quantities. A photocopy should be under five cents. Yet the impact is dramatic.

The ideal situation is to get your client to provide you a ream of their letterhead. You can offer to buy it from them at their cost, which is much less than if you produce it. This is only advised if you have a very strong relationship with your client. And it's particularly important if the client's letterhead has a custom watermark, embossing, or foil in their logo. The cost of reproduction would be prohibitive otherwise.

PUBLICITY REPRINTS

Print is the easiest publicity to preserve. You simply take the article and have it pasted up for reprints. If you don't know a pasteup artist, then almost any quick printer can do this for you. The articles are often in odd sizes, so you want it to fit on a standard 8½″ × 11″ sheet of paper. This format is the most economical to use later in your marketing program. Make sure that the publication masthead is at the top. For example, let's say you get an article in the *Columbus Dispatch*. Take the logotype from the front page and place it at the top of your article. You'll probably have to reduce the logotype to fit. This ensures that the recipient knows where the article came from. It's especially beneficial when the publication is well known to your target audience.

If the article is too big to fit on one sheet of paper, print on the back or on a second sheet. This is probably not necessary. Simply edit sections of the article that are of lesser importance so that it will fit on the 8½″ × 11″ paper. Most prospective clients won't read the entire article. Usually they only glance at it briefly, so you only need a good representation of the article. If they want the entire article, you can always provide them a copy. It won't be necessary too often, if at all.

After about twelve months you may want to consider masking out the date of the article. A good article, from a marketing standpoint, can last a lifetime. Take out specific elements that change dramatically with time, including fees. Simply brush some correction fluid (Wite-Out) lightly over the telltale numbers. It will look like a printing error and the numbers won't be legible. This is important when fees change over the years.

You can make greater impact with your publicity reprints by having them done on a gloss paper. The cost of the paper adds only a few cents to the cost of reproduction. If the article appeared in a magazine, you can have the masthead reproduced in a second color, much the same way the testimonials were reproduced. Again, the second color more than doubles the cost but it may be worth it.

Some articles are done in full color. Reproduction is usually out of the question because of the cost. Some magazines will reproduce them for you and they can be reasonable. It's a judgment call on your part.

Broadcast interviews are more difficult to document. One way is to be photographed during the interview or with the celebrity. Sometimes you'll get a thank-you letter from the celebrity or producer of the show. I received such a thank-you letter from Chris Cain, who interviewed me on CNN. You need to collect documentation that will fit well on an 8½" × 11" sheet of paper: the photo combined with an ad or promotional piece from the show, etc. You need just enough to illustrate your involvement.

When doing broadcast (or cablecast) either live or taped, make sure you bring your own blank tape. Get a copy of the interview. This may come in handy later for creating a promotional video- or audiotape.

If you would like to see the Streetfighter info kit, send $10 to Info Kit, Streetfighter Marketing, 467 Waterbury Ct., Gahanna, OH 43230. By the way, the ten bucks, when you consider postage and handling, is our cost in the thing.

Getting Prospects to Give You Referrals

That last thing we did in our conversation was to ask the prospect for referrals. Conventional wisdom would have you get referrals only from satisfied customers. That is fine, but just think how many referrals you would get when you get them from your prospects. After all, you probably have a hundred times as many prospects and dozens of times more qualified leads as you do satisfied customers.

Bill Bishop suggests that just because they have not bought from you yet, there is no reason why you could not ask for leads. You'll probably find that your prospects know other people like them who probably would be in the market for your products and services. So why wait? Ask now.

Bill points out further that it is just as important to ask in the right way. The question was not "Do you know anyone?" but rather, "Who do you know?" The appropriate responses to those two questions are far different. The first asks for a "yes" or a "no" answer. The second one is asking for the name of a possible referral.

After a name is given, you go on to qualify this lead as much as you can. "Why do you recommend this person?" gives you a little more information and helps you get a clearer picture of this potential new prospect before you even make the initial phone call.

Then you get permission to use your prospect's name. "When I call Mr. Robinson, is there any reason that I shouldn't mention your name?" It is always prudent to be sure.

Then when you are done, you repeat the process. "And who else do you know...?" Do this until the prospect runs out of names. Some prospects may have one or two names and some may have none. You may even get a prospect with a lot of names. But if you don't ask, you don't get!

Before you are done, you thank your prospect for the referrals and you "promise" to contact them right away. The reason you do this is that when calling your leads, you can start with "I promised Mr. Smith I'd call you right away." It gives a real sense of urgency and importance and helps you get the opportunity to present.

Referrals are much better than cold calls. If you work this part of your marketing program properly, after a time you may never have to make another cold call again. You could spend all your time just following up referrals. And you know that referrals make much more promising leads than cold calls.

The Presentation

Asking questions, not pitching features, is the way to uncover the real needs and problems of your prospect, which in turn allows you to offer your solutions. Your opening is a quick review of your first conversation. This helps you reinforce important points that you have discovered in your initial contact to make sure you are both on the same wavelength. You cannot assume anything in the follow-up contact. If you use a piece of important information from the first contact to make a point now, you can get yourself into trouble if your prospect changes his or her mind about that item.

For example, let's say you are selling a photocopy machine. In the first phone call, your prospect tells you they need a machine that has automatic feed, collates, and does two hundred pages a minute. You open your meeting telling your prospect about the perfect machine that has automatic feed, collates, and does two hundred pages a minute . . . and you start going into your pitch on this machine.

Then the prospect interrupts you in the middle of your wonderful pitch only to tell you that the boss decided they didn't need a collator but had to have a machine that copies in two colors. Your pitch is dead, and you have lost credibility by trying to sell something they cannot use. So review key points first so you can make midcourse corrections.

The brief review follows along the lines of "as you'll recall." Then you get agreement on the key points. For example: "As I recall, John, you need a machine that has an automatic feed, collates, and copies two hundred pages a minute. Is that right?" By asking for confirmation, you keep in control of the conversation and set the groundwork for your presentation.

Now, let's say the client gives you the new criteria. You can requalify on budget and other items and then go into the presentation about the machine that is most appropriate for your prospect's needs. You also want to subtly double-check the prospect's needs. After all, he did change on you once before, so you have to make sure that this is exactly what they need. No surprises.

If you are right, you will have reinforced it. If for some reason you are off base, you get an opportunity to make an important midcourse correction before you blow the entire presentation.

After you get agreement on the key points you have just reviewed, you must set the ground rules for the rest of the meeting. Tell your prospect that the purpose of your meeting or call today is to provide more information and background about the product or service that you offer. Then you want to turn it over to the prospect to find out more about his or her interests. Next, based on the conversation, you make a recommendation that the prospect may either approve or (pause as if to search for the right word) *im*prove upon. "Okay?"

With a response to your question, "Okay?" your prospect knows what to expect, and then the prospect has a turn to talk and ask questions. The prospect has also agreed to make a decision at the end of the conversation!

And if your prospect is not in a position to render a decision, you find that out so you can proceed accordingly.

As mentioned before, the term "presentation" may be a little misleading because you are going to listen more than you talk. By this time, you have a feel for what your client wants. Now you play "what if." Once the prospect tells you what he or she wants, you feed it back in the form of a "what if" statement.

For example, the client says, "I need an investment that'll give me a decent return but without a lot of risk." Most salespeople might respond with "Oh, great. I have this investment right here that'll do just that." This gives the prospect the opportunity to say, "Okay, let me think about it, and I'll get back to you."

However, if you respond with an "if/then" statement followed by a trial closing question, your prospect is more likely to agree with you. Therefore, you respond with "Well, John, *if* this program right here could offer you a good return on your investment with minimal risk, *then* would you want to take advantage of it today?"

Asking that question allows you to find out if the prospect is serious or not, because, once he or she says yes, your chances of getting the sale, once you satisfy the needs, are much greater.

You might even play with a little more aggressive version of the same game. "Well, John, if this program right here offers you a good return on your investment with minimal risk, you would want to take advantage of it...wouldn't you?" I have used both approaches and they both seem to work well, so pick the one that feels comfortable to you.

A hospital marketing maternity care might say, "So if I understand what you're saying, Mrs. Smith, if you found a hospital that offered a relaxed and comfortable child birthing center, with more flexible hours for family members, and top-notch round-the-clock medical staff, then you'd want to sign up for that hospital right away. Is that what you're telling me?"

An attorney might say, "So if I understand what you're telling me, if you found a law firm that could handle your work, explain everything to you in plain English, didn't nickel-and-dime you to death, and returned your phone calls promptly, you'd agree to work with that firm. Is that what you're telling me?"

If the prospect buys, then you are home free; but, in all likelihood, you will find that you are not quite there yet. You need a little more contact. After all, the client has not met you in person yet, and has only talked to you twice on the phone.

Dealing With Procrastinators and Handling Objections

Objections are ways your prospect delays making a decision. Your prospect may come up with one objection after another. Some of them will be reasonable and some are just downright crazy. Dealing with objections is an integral part of the selling process. In this section you learn why people procrastinate and how you can get them to make a decision.

Decision making is painful. When people are forced to make a decision, they feel pain and therefore use objections as a way of postponing the pain. You help the prospect to make decisions while keeping the pain to a minimum. When you have to make up your mind about something, your brain tells you that you are in pain. Think of the last time you had to make a major decision like buying a car or a house. It hurt. You racked your brain.

That is a very normal feeling. Bill Bishop, in his audio album *Million Dollar Presentations*, describes studies that were conducted to prove this point. Subjects were electronically monitored. During the experiment, the subjects were first pricked with a hatpin. Naturally they screamed. It hurt. It is amazing what college kids will do for a few extra bucks. Those brain waves were monitored on a computer. Later in the experiment, the subjects were forced to make some kind of decision. At this point, the brain waves showed the same response as they had with physical pain. Regardless of which decision was made, whether it was right or wrong, the pain immediately subsided as soon as the decision was made.

The point is that decision making is painful. So when you are asking your customers to make a decision about buying your products or services, they feel pain. And when you feel pain, your natural reaction is to do whatever you can to stop the pain. In the case of decision making, they want to postpone their decision. They do this with classic procrastination tactics like, "I want to think about it."

How to Create a Sense of Urgency. With procrastinating prospects, it is important to demonstrate not only the benefits of your product but also the importance of buying your product now. You must create a sense of urgency to get your procrastinator to a decision-making stage.

Price, availability, and loss of opportunity are perhaps used the most to create urgency. For example, a real estate opportunity could be lost because somebody else has interest in the same property. That is exactly what happened when my wife, Jodi, and I were buying our first home. We had just started looking but were in no rush. We knew we wanted to buy a home sometime in the next six months or so, but we were in no rush. We wanted to find the right one for us and at the right price. We figured, since we were in no hurry, we might just stumble into a bargain.

Low and behold, a friend of a friend knows about a house not even listed yet. We go see it. It is perfect. Needs no work and is underpriced. It turns out the owners bought another house which was costing them a fortune and they had to get out of the old house. We made an offer that night, knowing well and good that we would have paid full price on the house if we had to.

The next morning was when they first officially showed the house. Prior to that, however, they made us a counteroffer. I was going to counter again when I found out, through a very reliable source, that four other contracts were being drawn up and a few at full price. We accepted their offer right on the spot and bought the house.

Now, I was figuring to have a few more offers and counteroffer sessions, yet I jumped at their first counteroffer because I felt that I'd lose altogether if I did not. They created a sense of urgency that forced me to act immediately and pay a little more than I thought I had to.

As it turned out, there were indeed two contracts written on the house at full price. Regardless, it was the sense of urgency that caused us to make the single best financial decision we had ever made and make it fast.

Along the same lines, stock prices can go up at a moment's notice, so your prospect has to act before it is too late. A disaster could happen at any moment, leaving your prospect's family unprotected; so it is imperative that the insurance policy get immediate approval. Your prospect's business is losing the money- and time-saving benefits of not having your computer or telecommunications system installed right now, plus you expect a 10 percent price increase very soon.

So when you are selling your clients, you are actually

selling them on making two different decisions. The first is the value in buying your products and services. The follow-up is the value in buying now.

The Four Steps to Converting Objections

To effectively handle objections, use the Street Smart four-step approach:

1. Soften
2. Isolate
3. Rephrase
4. Suggest a solution

No matter how good you are at qualifying and bringing your clients along in the marketing process, there are bound to be some objections. Some are valid, others not so valid, but you have to deal with these objections and bring your client to the commitment stage.

Now you will discover the real reasons people fire objection after objection at you. You then learn how to handle those objections effectively. You also learn about the four steps to handling an objection: soften, isolate, rephrase, and suggest. And finally, you will learn how to go right from the objection into the close of the sale.

Objections are really good. They show that your prospect has interest enough in what you are offering to ask questions. But, as you have learned many times before, the person who asks the questions controls the conversation.

First, you have to determine the level of objection. For example, you are selling a car and your prospect tells you, "I really like it, but do you have it in green?"

At this point you do not know if green is a "make it or

break it" element to the sale. The prospect may be just making conversation. If you do not have it in green, you have opened yourself up to a "Well, let me think about it, and I'll get back to you." So when you hear, "Do you have it in green?" simply respond with "Do you want it in green?" To which you will probably get: "Oh, not really, I was just wondering."

Expand that example slightly and imagine that you know you do not have it in green, but you do not want to open yourself up. If you respond with "Do you want it in green?" you have given your prospect an opportunity to say, "Sure, I'd love it in green." And then you are in trouble.

So if you do not have the exact one you have just been asked about, you need to find out if it can make or break the deal. So you ask this question: "Is that important to you?"

This direct question lets you know exactly where your prospect stands on that issue. Your prospect might come back with "Oh, not real important. Do you have it in red?"

Another possible response is, "Interesting question, why do you ask?"

Objections can be annoying at times. What they are probably doing at this point is postponing that decision. Remember. . . it is painful. So when you start to come up with objections that sound like the prospect is running a little scared, use the four-step approach to objections: soften, isolate, rephrase, and suggest.

Soften. This first step is real easy. No matter what your prospect tells you . . . no matter how crazy the objection is, you simply respond with "I understand."

So if the prospect says, "I really want it in red," you respond first with "I understand."

You see, consumers have been conditioned to be on

their guard whenever they talk to anyone that remotely sounds like a salesperson. They know that as soon as they offer an objection, many salespeople try to wear them down to buy. It is often a big confrontation between the salesperson and the client.

Isolate. Your second step is called "isolate." Your prospect may have numerous objections subconsciously tucked away in the back of his head that he is saving for the moment you ask him to make a decision. Here, he automatically springs objection after objection on you. I am sure you have experienced this, and you know how frustrating it is. You have spent a lot of time and talent helping the prospect to understand that the objection really is not a reason not to commit. After having successfully dealt with that objection, that prospect comes back with "yes, but," and you have to start all over again.

To break the response chain of having to answer one objection after another, you isolate the objection by asking a simple question. "Other than [insert objection], is there any reason that we can't get the go-ahead with this right now?"

By "isolating" the objection, your prospect has told you that this is the *only* reason for not making a decision now. Notice how this technique enables your prospect to agree, and if this one and only objection is dealt with, the prospect gives you the go-ahead.

It also helps to avoid painful words that put prospects on alert like "sign" or "contract." Instead, use nonthreatening terminology like, "Let's give it the go-ahead," "get the ball rolling," or "give it a try." Rather than signing, you might ask for his "approval." "Contracts" become the "paperwork." These words and phrases are informal and, consequently, make the decision-making process less painful.

It is a good rule of thumb to assume that, in your prospect's mind, anything he or she says is true, but anything you say to the prospect is suspect. In order for the prospect to believe what you are saying, you get the prospect to say it for you. You do this by guiding your prospect along with leading questions in much the same way as a psychologist would help someone with a problem to discover the answer for himself or herself.

The point is, by asking questions, especially during the objection phase, you not only control the conversation but create an atmosphere where the prospect discovers for himself or herself the solution to the problem.

Now, let's tie this back into isolating the objection. By getting the prospect to agree that a particular objection is the only thing standing between you and the sale, it becomes very difficult for that prospect to come back with another objection later.

Rephrase. The next step is to rephrase the objection into a format that you can deal with. For example, your prospect says, "I cannot afford it." That is a statement. It is very final, but you cannot answer a statement. You can only answer a question, so you have to get the prospect to agree that the statement that was just made was actually a question so that you can then offer an answer to that question.

You cannot debate "affordability," but you can discuss "cost" and "value." To illustrate, consider this. Your prospect says, "Well, I cannot afford it." You might respond, "I understand . . . so what you are telling me, Mary, is that it costs too much. Is that your question?" Even though she did not ask it as a question, refer to it as if she did. It is very difficult to deal with a question of affordability because what some can afford is oftentimes a judgment call. What they are really saying is that they have not yet been convinced that what you have to offer has value enough to justify the expenditure.

"Cost" rather than affordability, on the other hand, is

an entirely different matter. Cost is not an arbitrary judgment call, but a quantitative amount. Cost is something you can deal with. So not only do you convert the objection from a statement to a question, but you also rephrase it in a way that you can answer.

Let's take another example. Your prospect might say, "I do not believe in life insurance." Now, you can attack your prospect and try to prove that he or she is wrong. When you attack, keep in mind that psychologists tell us that there are usually only two natural responses: fight or flight. Either response puts us in a bad position to set up the close of a sale.

Psychologists also tell us that there are only four basic emotions: mad, sad, glad, and scared. The only time a prospect agrees to buy is when he or she is glad.

Keeping this in mind, you then simply rephrase it into a question. You respond with something like, "So, if I understand you correctly, Ms. Ritz, you think life insurance is not a sound investment. Is that your question?"

Again, notice how I restate the prospect's statement. It is difficult to deal with what someone believes in. Yet, once Ms. Ritz agrees that what she really meant was that she does not think life insurance is a sound investment, I have something I can discuss with her. Furthermore, by tacking on "Is that your question?" I am given an opportunity to prove it is a sound investment which I am more than prepared to deal with.

How to Offer Your Suggested Solution. Next, you isolate one more time to make sure you are in a position to close. But before you do, you tie in some key information from the initial discovery that was conducted in your first two phone calls. Let's assume that in those first two phone calls, our prospect's biggest financial concern is putting her two daughters through school.

You respond with "Let me ask you this. If I could

prove to you, right here and now, that we have a program available that provides a strong return on your investment and guarantees you that, regardless of what happens to you, your two daughters will be able to go to college, would you give me the go-ahead on it?"

Once I get her "yes" on my hypothetical situation, the prospect has agreed to buy provided that her specific needs are met. Reaching a specific financial goal is something that every insurance agent is trained to do. So it is a relatively easy process from here... provided you do not give your prospect any more ammunition to object again.

If you put it all together, it should flow right along. Let's use an advertising media salesperson representing a trade magazine who is calling on a small manufacturer as our example to illustrate this flow.

"Well, we really cannot afford to advertise in your magazine right now... Perhaps in the next quarter we might be able to do something."

"I understand. Other than the cost of the ad, is there anything else that would keep you from placing your ad in the next issue?"

"No, not really, but our cash flow is just awful right now, and we just do not want to tie ourselves down at this time."

"I see. So if I understand you correctly, you really would like to get into our next issue, it is just that you do not have the ready cash. Is that your question?"

"That's it in a nutshell. Even though this is our busy season for new orders, we don't start getting paid on those for probably... oh, ninety days out. That's the one thing I hate about this business."

"Let me ask you this. How much could you realistically afford... the amount that you would not even have to think about to give me the go-ahead?"

"Gee, I don't know. Maybe about half the budget?"

"So if I could show you how to place your ad in time to hit your busy season for half this amount, you'd do it. Is that what I am hearing?"

"Sure, but how can you do that?"

"Are you familiar with our special Peak Time Protection Plan?"

"No, I don't believe so."

"Well, it very simply states that we understand your situation, and we can provide a payment program that allows you to advertise when you need to and pay when you get the results."

Of course, if there was no special credit program, you would come up with another strategy helping the prospect understand just how valuable the product or service is. The other option might be to offer a smaller ad that would fit in the budget which he already told you he *could* afford.

So remember these four steps to dealing with objections: The first is to soften. No matter what they say, you immediately follow up with "I understand."

Step two is to isolate the objection. You do this by asking, "Other than [objection], is there any other reason that we could not get the go-ahead right now?"

Step three is to restate the objection as a question that you can answer. "So if I understand you correctly, you think [and you rephrase the objection]." Then follow it with "Is that your question?"

Finally the customer has agreed that he or she wants you to answer the question, and you can deal in one and only one issue to get close to the point of commitment.

Controlling Objections Before They Become Objections

The best way to handle an objection is to deal with it

before it becomes an objection. Many objections that prospects throw out to salespeople are given to them by the salesperson. It goes right back to salespeople volunteering too much information, not asking questions, and *not* listening to the customer.

If you get an objection repeatedly, you need to find a way to deal with it before it becomes a problem in your sales process. In the Introduction of this book, you read a brief mention of Bob Kramer, the successful Midwest sewing machine retailer who used the telephone to generate new customers. Besides getting customers in to try out the new computerized machines, he also used the phone another way.

Every year his store offered several classes and seminars on sewing techniques. This was not only a nice revenue generator for him but got people to his store, which indirectly got more machine sales as well. The primary medium to fill a seminar or class had been direct mail, but the results started sagging in the past few years so he tried using the phone.

He started by calling his customer base and conducting a survey to see what types of classes and seminars they would be interested in. He prompted them for a list of programs that were available to him. When he figured out which would be the most popular, he created a schedule for the classes. Then he started calling once again to try to fill each class.

Early on in the phone calls, he noticed that people were a little hesitant to commit to a class, for it meant giving him a credit card number over the phone to reserve their seat. They would usually use the objection that they were not available on that date. After a few of these objections, he changed his presentation.

This time when he called, one of the first questions he would ask before he got too far into the conversation was their availability on these dates. At that point in the conversation he was not asking for a commitment, so the vast majority of the potential attendees, provided they were available, said that they were. Once they had said that they had no schedule conflict, they could not come back later in the presentation and say that they did. It alleviated the objection before it became an objection.

It is like the old joke. Just before they go to bed, the husband brings his wife a glass of water and two aspirin. She looks at him and says, "I do not have a headache." There is no way that objection could be used later!

Doubling Your Results on the Phone

For most of us, marketing is not a full-time job. It has to be done to make sure we have a lucrative business or practice. It also has to be done in a minimal amount of time, since, as a rule, we can only devote a limited amount of time to it. Therefore, it is vital that you incorporate ways to get the most of the time you do allocate for your marketing program.

Regardless of the level of your sales skills, selling is a numbers game. Selling by telephone is even more so. The more calls you make, the more sales you get. Therefore, in order for you to get the maximum number of appointments from your marketing efforts, you must look for every possible way to make the best use of your prime telephone calling time. This allows you to get the most clients for your efforts.

Accurately tracking the results of your telephone selling activities helps you make improvements in all aspects of your marketing program. Lesson number one for increasing your sales by telephone is: Do not waste valuable telephone time doing tasks that could have been done at another time or, better yet, by someone else. If you are selling business services, for example, your peak selling hours are between 9:00 A.M. and 5:00 P.M., so you want to spend as much of that time as possible on the phone. Selling life insurance to a married couple may mean that your prime selling time is in the evening when most people are home from work (6:00 to 9:00 P.M.)—or perhaps on weekends. So the first thing you have to do is figure out when *your* prime selling time is. Then determine how many total hours you have in a given day or week to actually make calls.

Set aside specific hours for your phone calling. If you're going to call three hours a day, three days a week, mark it off your calendar so it won't be disturbed. Consider calling from your home or a hotel room if need be so that you won't be interrupted.

By tracking your calling efforts, you may also discover that, even though theoretically your prime calling time is 9:00 to 5:00 Monday through Friday, not all days are created equal when it comes to getting through to your prospects. You may find through this tracking that Monday morning and Friday afternoons yield poorer results than all the other available days and day parts. So you may define your prime calling time as Tuesdays through Thursdays 9:00 to 5:00, Mondays 1:00 to 5:00, and Fridays 9:00 to noon.

You also want to keep in mind that when there is a three-day holiday weekend, the Thursday afternoon before a Friday off or the Tuesday morning following a Monday off might be just as weak.

The reason you need to be aware of this is that you have only a certain number of hours during the day when you can effectively get through to the right people. If you have to run an errand or do research, you want to avoid doing that during those prime calling times.

If you know that certain times on certain days are strong for getting through to decision makers, you want to make sure you do not plan any other tasks then . . . but rather schedule them for a less valuable time slot.

Headsets. When spending a great deal of time on the phone, it is best to keep your hands free. To do this, consider getting a high-quality headset. It saves wear and tear on your neck. They come cordless and with a cord. The cordless sounds a little hollow, so it is better to use the corded one, which will cost in the $100–$150 range. Make sure you get a good one. A company called Plantronics has several different models that are excellent. I suggest you get on their mailing list.[29]

Phone Log Sheets. A phone log sheet is one simple way to track your phone calls. You will obviously want to adapt your log to best suit your specific needs. See the example on the following page.

Tracking information is very helpful to you in becoming a better salesperson. I am always looking for ways, especially gadgets, that can help me do just that. According to an article that appeared in *Direct Marketing Magazine:*

> It is wise to work within a structure that will produce quantitative and qualitative data for the applications to be pursued. The first step in the process is to look for numbers that might be used as norms. The key in estimating telemarketing costs lies with two sets of numbers: 1) cost per call for handling inbound calls from business firms and consumers, and 2) cost per call per decision-maker contact in making outbound calls to business firms and consumers. Work sheets can be

---

[29]Plantronics, 345 Encinal St., Santa Cruz, CA 95060-2132. (800) 538-0748; in California (800) 662-3902.

TELESELLING TELEPHONE DAILY LOG SHEET
Confidential—Do not remove from office

Date _____Salesperson _____Week of _____Total Dials _____

A—Cold call   E—Message returned
B—Qualified call back   F—Disqualified/killed
C—New lead qualified   G—Tickler File
D—Message left   H—Presentation delivered

	A	B	C	D	E	F	G	H
8:00								
9:00								
10:00								
11:00								
12:00								
1:00								
2:00								
3:00								
4:00								
5:00								
6:00								
7:00								
Total								

New Qualified Leads   Call Back Progress
(list new projects)   (list call backs)

                                                 (current status)

_____   _____   In Ex CP Dead*
_____   _____   In Ex CP Dead
_____   _____   In Ex CP Dead
_____   _____   In Ex CP Dead
_____   _____   In Ex CP Dead

Notes:

_____

* In = interested   CP   = contract pending
  Ex = excited   Dead = delete from file

developed for inbound and outbound costs. The process also involves: 1) using the sales call ratio advantage or telemarketing as a base to compare sales cost, 2) determining the present cost of acquiring new customers, 3) looking at the first-year results, 4) exploring the time compression potential as it relates to acquiring 1,000 new customers and 5) determining the chances for success.[30]

Wall Charts Display Qualified Lead Status. It often helps to see where you are by having a wall display that allows you to categorize your leads according to status. We use the following categories:

Qualified Lead
Requalified
Interested
Excited
Contract Pending
Sold
Dead

Of course you will want to change these categories to best suit your particular needs and setup. The challenge is to be able to move the card with the appropriate information to the proper category. Just writing the prospect name on an erasable chart does not really work because as soon as that prospect's status changes, either up or down, it is difficult to keep your system up-to-date. Therefore, you need a system where each lead is placed on its own card. It sounds easy but we experimented with a number of different ways until we found a few that would work well.

---

[30] "The Mathematics of Telemarketing," by Bob Stone and John Wyman. *Direct Marketing Magazine* 49, no. 8 (December 1986), pp. 46–52.

Besides changing the status column easily, you can gain good insight into your progress by color coding the cards by month. By color coding the month, when you start putting up your qualified leads on your status board, you can see at a glance not only how many leads you have for a given month but how fast they are progressing through the system.

In our organization, we use the ninety-day test for "decision mode." If prospects cannot make a decision in ninety days we put them in a tickler file until they can. By the same token, if a given lead does not change status within a reasonable amount of time, you need to be aware of it. So if I am looking at the status board in April and still see some blue cards, which means it was started last November, I know these leads are not moving fast enough. The idea is to move numerous quality leads through the sales system. Effective marketing relies on both the quality and the quantity of leads you work.

Index Card Filing System. The index card filing system from Caddylak Systems uses regular 3″ × 5″ index cards. The top inch or so of each card remains visible at all times for quick reference. It has eight columns holding twenty-eight cards each.

Computerize Your Marketing

The most effective thing you can do to track and follow up your marketing program is to put the entire process on computer. Though there are a couple of programs available for this, the one we're most familiar with and use in our office is called TeleMagic by Remote Control (see page 242). Provided you keep your contact files up-to-date with regards to the prospect status, and if you have a field specifically for status, you can create a filter that allows you to print out a report, as often as you like, of all the prospects in certain categories.

Once you're using a computer for your marketing, your next step will be to network your computers. This is important because you'll find that a number of people in your operation will use the TeleMagic software and it will probably be on a number of different machines. This causes a small problem.

One of the advantages of using computer software is that with a few keystrokes you have all the information you need about a client. However, a change, deletion, or addition to one computer file isn't automatically carried through to others. To solve this problem, you need to network your computers. Our experience has been that we found it absolutely necessary to do this after two years with our computer system. In retrospect we wish we would have done it from the beginning.

The system we recommend is the one we know most about. It's called Novell® and is the most widely used network system available.[31] Novell is also the most stable company providing local area networking, with annual sales of $421.9 million in 1989. Novell's flagship product, Netware® (version 2.2), is what we use in our office. It has tremendous capabilities, is easy to learn, and we found the support people at Novell to be extremely helpful.

You can set up for any amount of users you wish. It allows every user to share one data base, which was the main capability we were looking for. In this way, if a change is made to any file, every person in the office has that change. The networking also has some other benefits we didn't even count on. It lets us share

---

[31] Novell, Inc., 122 E. 1700 South, Provo, UT 84606. (800) 453-1267; (801) 429-7000.

printers with any station and allows us to have some great backup functions.

The system does much more than that and you may find that having a network will be of value with other software you run. It's worth investigating.

CHAPTER 11

When Advertising Makes Sense and How to Do It for Less

Sometimes it does make sense to advertise. In this chapter you'll get a brief overview of the different advertising media as well as a few "inside" tricks for buying it for less and making it more effective.

Newspaper: More Than Wrapping Fish

Newspaper is one of the most widely used forms of advertising. It's also one of the most costly. In most markets there is only one daily newspaper. It's a monopoly, and as a result the price of newspaper advertising is high. At the same time it's the only game in town for many advertisers. Despite the price, it's critical that you track results from your newspaper advertising (and for any advertising, for that matter) to see what your return on investment is.

A standard newspaper is nine columns wide by twenty-two inches tall. You're charged for the amount of space you use. This can be done in column inches or figured in "lines." Regardless, the size of the ad determines the cost of the ad. So the game is to figure out the smallest ad you need to get the job done.

There have been tests conducted (usually sponsored by broadcast advertisers) that contend that a 2/3-page ad has about an 11 percent readership while a 1/3-page ad has about an 8 percent readership. The smaller of the two ads only loses 3 percent readership while the cost is half. Can we believe these numbers? It's been said that advertising people use statistics like a drunk uses a lamppost . . . more for support than illumination. Common sense tells us that there is probably some truth in this claim. It may or may not be to the degree stated, but the claim does seem to make sense.

Benefit Headlines Are Critical. Your newspaper ad needs to have a benefit headline that grabs the attention of the reader. It also needs strong body copy to cause the reader to finish the ad. Lastly the ad must ask the reader to take action.

I was working with a podiatrist in West Virginia who was spending well over $100,000 a year in advertising and not getting the results he needed. After I looked through the ads the problem was obvious. The local paper was helping him create his ads and used "cutsie" headlines like "Put Your Best Foot Forward" or "Time to Put Your Foot Down." They were cute plays on words yet provided absolutely no benefit to the reader. Besides, there was a lot of clip art of feet and legs that also gave little benefit.

As I looked over the ads, I saw near the bottom, in very small type: "Free Foot Exam." Here was the benefit and it was hidden. So I cut the size of the ad by half, took the "Free Foot Exam" and made it the headline, and created a subheadline and some body copy that reinforced this doctor's credibility as a podiatrist. Then his photo was used in the ad as well, to give additional credibility to the doctor. The same approach was also used in his TV and radio ads. Lastly there was a number to call for the free appointment.

The ad worked. I think the reason it worked, despite the smaller size, was that the headline offered the reader a powerful benefit. Not fancy. Not cutsie. One of the most successful headlines ever used is "Hemorrhoids." If you've got them you'll read the ad, and if you don't you won't. But it doesn't matter.

Oftentimes there's a desire to put the name of the organization in the headline. You'll probably get stronger results if you put the name of the business last. Give readers a reason to read the ad first. Then show them where they can get those benefits.

To test your ads, you might consider having the reader make a telephone call. This two-step process can be very effective. The ad creates a demand—now. If they don't take action immediately, the chance of their doing it later is diminished. It continues to diminish the longer they wait until they totally forget or lose the desire to call you. The testing comes into play by giving the caller a special extension number. The extension number changes from ad to ad. These numbers tell you which ad got the response. The person in your office receiving the phone calls needs to track these numbers so you know which ads pulled and which didn't.

Besides the size and content of the ads, other variables that determine an ad's success include position and section in the paper, day of the week, and even the weather. These elements should be considered when trying to determine the success of an ad.

Once you get a successful ad, stick with it. Don't change just to be changing it. Mr. Whipple and Ring

Around the Collar have been successful for decades. Most likely you won't be spending hundreds of thousands of dollars on media in your marketplace. It takes a lot of frequency before people get tired of your ad. You'll get tired of it first. Your friends and family second. However, they're not the ones you want as clients, so don't listen to them. Stick with success.

If you're going to spend money in the newspaper, it's probably a good idea to get a strong layout artist and copywriter to help you with your ad. It should look professional and clean and sell the main points. Be careful of the overly creative types who would rather win awards than get results. Look at their portfolios and see the ads they do. Then ask about the results of the ads. Some of the best award winners didn't necessarily get results. There's an old adage in the advertising business, "It's only creative if it sells."

Newspaper Alternatives. There are usually several tabloids or specialty newspapers available in a market. If you're tempted to use them, be sure to track results very carefully. Though the cost is a fraction of the daily newspaper, it's not likely to get the same results and may give you the wrong image in the marketplace. A tabloid or neighborhood paper doesn't have to get the same results. You need to look at the return on your investment. How much did the ad cost you? How much revenue did it bring in? The ratio is the only fair way to compare a smaller medium with the larger one.

If you're tempted to use a full page, consider using the "Streetfighters Cheater's Page." Instead of the full nine columns by twenty-two inches, try eight columns by eighteen inches. You won't lose any readership yet will save 10 to 15 percent on the cost of the ad. The only exception to this is if the full page puts you on the back page of the section. Back-page placement gets much more readership.

You can even save more money by going with the "Streetfighters Dominant Ad." This is an ad that is five columns wide by fourteen inches tall. It makes you the dominant ad on the page and no one can have a bigger ad. It also places your headline above the centerfold so it's more likely to get read.

The newspaper lets you choose the section, so choose one that appeals to your potential customers. Sports scale more toward men. "Accent" scales more to women. Obituaries scale older. Business is obvious.

Classified can be a very inexpensive way to target by need. Classified advertising, like the yellow pages, is one of the few advertising media where the buyer is looking specifically for the ads. They're in the market to buy.

One of my favorite examples of the power of newspaper advertising was first written in our first book, *Streetfighting*. When I was in college, I became one of a dozen student directors of our Student Union building at Indiana University. It was our responsibility to provide programming at the Union for the student body. One of the major programming areas was movies.

At the beginning of each semester we had a special event in the Union called "Dusk Till Dawn" where the biggest attraction was nonstop free movies. To promote this event, we would run a full-page ad on the back page of the student newspaper. The headline was done in a very thin, block-type style and read, "FREE FLICKS." It was a strong benefit headline that in itself should have attracted many students to the program.

But this one semester we had an unusually high turnout. When the ad was created, it looked beautiful. On the art board it looked elegant. The problem was that newsprint tends to absorb a little. The letters in the headline were very close together, and when the ad ran, the "L" and the "I" in the word FLICKS bled together to form what looked like a "U." No one seemed disappointed, though, when all they got was a free movie!

Broadcast: Costs, Controls, and Consequences

TV is another very powerful medium but very costly in most markets. You have some options with TV. First there are usually at least three network affiliates plus an independent or two. Usually the independents are cheaper, but you have to go by the audience size to determine what you're getting for the money paid.

TV stations (and radio too) usually set their rates based on ratings. There are two types of ratings. The first is called the "share." This is the percentage of TV households watching TV tuned to a particular show. A 25 percent share means that one fourth of all those people watching TV are tuned to that show.

The "rating point" refers to the percentage of all TV households in the area tuned to a show. A rating of 10 points means that 10 percent of the total TV households are watching that show.

Now that you know what they mean . . . forget them. For smaller budgets it's worthless. The best way you can figure out what you're going to get is by using a term called "cost per thousand," or CPM. The rating books can tell you how many thousands of viewers are watching a given show. They can also narrow it down by sex and age. For example, if your target audience is primarily men between ages eighteen and thirty-four or women over fifty-four you can find the shows that appeal to that age group. Though there might be other shows that get a much bigger overall audience, you're only concerned about what it costs you to reach the people likely to become your clients.

Then you take the cost of the commercial time or "spot" against the targeted audience, and you find out what it costs to reach each one thousand people in our target audience. A CPM of twenty-five dollars for total adults eighteen to fifty-four means it costs you twenty-five dollars to reach each one thousand men and women between the ages of eighteen and fifty-four. Your station account executive or rep can help you figure your CPMs, but make sure that he or she is doing it for the correct target audience and is using the most current statistics available. Most stations subscribe to two rating services: Arbitron and Nielsen. The rating books come out periodically. When comparing shows and stations, make sure you use the same rating service and the same rating book.

Spot Length. The length of your commercial can vary. There are 60s, 30s, 10s, and more recently 15s. Each of these numbers stands for the seconds. Generally a 60-second spot costs exactly twice that of a 30-second spot. A 10-second spot costs half a 30, so you're paying a premium for the spot. Use the shortest commercial you need to make your point.

Producing an Ad. Locally produced ads are usually pretty obvious. If you are trying to build credibility for your business, practice, product, or service, you have to be very sensitive to not coming off hokey or cheap in your ad. At the same time quality television production can be very expensive.

One way to amortize the cost is to create a "donut." This is a generic open and close to your ad, perhaps the first and last five to seven seconds. It's done very professionally and you put a little money behind it. You can change the "hole," or middle part, to promote specifics. This gives you much flexibility and can be used for years.

The unseen announcer in an ad is called the "voice-over." This means you're watching a visual but not the person speaking. Use a professional announcer for your voice-over. It won't cost you that much more but really sets the tone. Voice talent varies widely, so search for one that creates the right image for you. You don't want to come off sounding like a used-car salesman (especially if you are one). Be professional and dignified and share the benefits with the viewers.

Commercials shot with videotape instead of film look local. Film is prohibitively expensive for local production. One way around this, if your concept permits, is to use quality still photography. Then, in-studio, the cameras do slow pans, zooms, and dissolves from one photo to the next. Add a quality voice-over and your production can look network quality on a local budget.

Negotiating Airtime. Airtime is a perishable commodity, and as a result it is negotiable based on supply and demand. When demand is high, like around Christmas, you'll pay the rate card. When demand is low, like January or summer, you stand a better chance of negotiating a more favorable deal with the station.

You can buy a specific show which is called a "fixed position." You'll pay more for that. Another way to go is to buy a "rotator." This spot can fall anywhere between the two times selected. For example, you might buy a rotator between 6:00 and 11:00 P.M. This means that they can put your spot anytime between the early and late news, which means that it might end up in prime time or prime access just before 8:00. It's a little bit of a gamble, but if demand is low, you have a good chance at getting some of your spots to fall into the stronger times.

When negotiating it is best to set your budget up front and let the station rep come back to you with a proposal. Let's say you have set aside a budget of $5,000.

When the rep returns, you wouldn't try to get that schedule for $4,500, but rather try to get more spots for the money. Keep the $5,000 static. The rep is paid a percentage of the sale. If you try to drop your budget, it's money out of the rep's pocket and he's not excited about giving up that money. On the other hand, he'll give you as much as he can get away with to get that order.

Sometimes he'll throw in some free spots after 11:00 P.M. or give you a few extra 10s or tighten the bracket on a rotator from 4:00–11:00 to 7:00–11:00 that automatically guarantees you a bigger audience.

Having a good relationship with a creative TV rep can be very beneficial, and he or she will show you how to get the most out of his/her station.

Frequency vs. Reach. There is an ongoing debate about reach and frequency. "Reach" refers to the size of the audience, while "frequency" refers to the number of spots you get. On small budgets I feel it's to your advantage to go for frequency. The more times the same person sees (or hears) your commercial, the higher the likelihood of action being taken. You want the same person to see your spot at least 6 times. It does you little good to have a large audience see your spot once or twice. I think you're better off reaching a smaller audience but reaching them often.

Opportunity Program Buying. There is an idea we call "opportunity program buying" that dramatically increases the impact of a few commercials. Look for a newscast or talk show with a subject that is directly related to your product or service. Then buy one commercial in each commercial break. For example, a real estate agent specializing in low-to-mid-range homes finds out that Donahue is covering the difficulty of young couples buying their first home. The content of the show creates the demand for your services. All you have to do is put a spot, perhaps just a ten-second spot, in each commercial break letting that audience know that you specialize in helping young couples get their first home. For little money you've made a big impact. I was always impressed by the cruise line that ran an ad on *The Love Boat*.

You really have to be aware of opportunities and be ready to spring into action at a moment's notice. Again, having a strong relationship with a media rep is helpful in uncovering these gems.

Radio. Radio is tremendously flexible and is often affordable. You have more variety of stations from which to choose and people have a tendency to listen to stations based on their format.

Beautiful music seems to scale older, while album-oriented rock (AOR) scales much younger. Top 40 and oldies scale in the middle and all-talk radio a little older. All the formats appeal to special types of groups and it's a good idea to look at the rating book to get an idea of which station reaches the audience you want. Caution: Don't buy the station *you* listen to unless you are the type of person who buys your services.

Radio production is a fraction of the cost of television, so you can have a very professionally produced radio spot for very little. Unless you're provided a jingle from a national supplier, don't bother doing one. You can't compete with the top-quality jingles out there. You'll only come off amateurish and spend a lot of money in the process.

In radio, a 60-second spot is only slightly more than a 30, so you might look at 60s. The spot cost is based on audience size, which is divided into day parts. They are:

Morning Drive	6–10
Daytime	10–4

Afternoon Drive	4–7
Night	7–midnight
Overnight	midnight–6

Morning and Afternoon Drive time, Monday through Friday, is the prime time in radio because that's when most people are driving to and from work. Daytime is usually a little smaller in size. Night time drops, and last, the Overnights are a very small audience.

Negotiation. Radio is generally more competitive than local TV. They'll work harder for a smaller amount of money and there are more stations out there trying to get it. Negotiate hard. Again, set your budget up front. Select the time slots you want, then when the rep comes back with the proposal, go for more spots. Leave the budget figure alone.

All things being equal, you might be better off putting your money into one or two stations instead of spreading it over four or five. The more money you spend on a given station, the more they'll fight for it and the larger the concessions. This plays stronger when it's a one-station buy and the competition gets cut out altogether.

A little hint. You may find that the number-one station is not the way to go. They're often arrogant about their number-one position and won't negotiate much as a result. You'll get much more cooperation from the second and third stations in the marketplace. Your cost per thousand will be lower. Remember, frequency is important, so get a lot of spots and dominate an audience instead of getting spread too thin.

Some stations will suggest you spread your schedule out over many weeks or over many day parts. Given a limited budget, you're better off concentrating your schedule to make greater impact. Buy only one or two day parts. Take a four-week schedule and pack it into ten days.

Short-term repetition makes impact, especially if you're not on all the time. Rule of thumb: When you're on, get on strong. If you can't afford to be on strong, stay off till you can.

Radio also has much more scheduling flexibility. Some stations will let you air your spots only during certain favorable conditions. For example, if you sell pools or pool supplies, people only think of you when it's sunny. So you arrange for the station to play your spots only when it's sunny. You'll get more impact from your schedule.

Outdoors: Convincing yet Costly

Billboards are very costly and harder to come by. Many communities are putting tough restrictions on billboards and signage. So there are fewer billboards available, which makes the ones out there sell for a premium.

The best way to use a billboard locally is as a directional. This is when the billboard directs the traffic to your location. "Left at next exit." Keep your billboard simple. Six words in the headline and only three elements in the board. A board that is too busy and hard to read is likely to get ignored. One of my favorite boards is for Red Roof Inns. It simply says, "Sleep Cheap!" Simple, memorable, effective.

The other way to buy billboards is "postings." They use a term called "gross rating points," or GRP. It's meaningless for your purposes so don't let them confuse you. All you have to know is how many boards you get for what price.

It was once suggested to me by a billboard account executive that to get more exposure for the money and if it's not critical that you be up twelve full months, you might try every other month for a year. When you go for twelve consecutive months, there's a small discount. However, by going every other month for a year you pay for only six months. Do they immediately run out the first day your board expires and replace it with a Seagram's ad? Sometimes yes and sometimes no. You're likely to find that you'll get the equivalent of 10 to 30 percent or more free exposure. I've had boards that stayed up for six months extra at no cost to me. Your production costs will be a little higher because you'll need more paper this way, but it might be worth it.

It even works better when you change locations for your boards on the months you're up.

There are alternatives to billboards like "Jr. Boards," bus shelters, benches, transit areas, and a host of others. For most people trying to build a customer base, other forms of outdoor advertising might be too hokey. Be careful.

Dueling Billboards. My favorite story about an effective use of billboards was done by a hair salon. They had a very successful business and built up a nice clientele. Their haircuts were priced at thirty dollars, so they were pretty upscale for this market. After a while a new shopping center was built directly across the street from this hair salon. In this shopping center went one of those discount haircut chains. To advertise this new discount salon, the owners bought the billboard in front of the shopping center. In a plain blue background and plain white letters with an arrow pointing directly into the center, they put "$6 Haircuts."

It was a very successful billboard. Strong benefit and direction at the same time. It started hurting the upscale salon across the street. How could they compete with this discounter? They'd developed a certain reputation and were charging a premium for their services. Price cutting to meet the competition would destroy their upscale position. They needed to come up with a way to reinforce their position. So they bought the billboard in front of their own salon. Using the same blue background and same plain white letters, they simply put, "We Fix $6 Haircuts." Turned them around instantly!

Yellow Pages: Should Your Finger Do the Talking?

The yellow pages are another must buy for many types of businesses. The key here, like the newspaper, is to buy as small an ad as you think you can get away with. Yellow pages advertising is very expensive, and you pay it out every month. To complicate matters, you can now buy spot color to enhance your ad. And to complicate matters even more, there are new publications trying to compete with the telephone companies' yellow pages.

The yellow pages are necessary for many service organizations. A client in need of something often looks in the yellow pages. The advantage is that such people are usually qualified buyers. On the other hand, yellow pages are one of the few advertising media that put you next to every competitor you have in the marketplace. That's why it's a good idea not to mention in your other advertising to look for your yellow-page ad.

Again, use a strong headline. This is critical. Also make sure the copy has strong benefits to the reader. The bigger the ad, the more it costs but the better the placement. Trying smaller ads is something you can test over the years, but do it gradually if you are used to having a bigger ad.

Don't let your yellow-page sales rep talk you into something you don't really want. They are the best high-pressure salespeople you'll ever hear and use fear very effectively in their presentation. Be prepared. Your ad is too important to have their people design it for you. With all the money you're likely to put into yellow-page advertising, pay a little more to have a professional design yours. With camera-ready art ready to go, it is really hard for the sales rep to push you into the next largest size.

Competitive Exit. Keep your eyes open for competition that goes under. There might be some opportunity for you. We wrote in our first book about someone who took advantage of such an opportunity. As a result, a private investigator did the same in Akron, Ohio. One of his competitors went out of business. That competitor had a yellow-page ad twice the size of his. He found out that the competitor used an answering service that owned the phone number. So he took over their nominal monthly service fee. His business doubled at hardly any cost to him.

Some of the yellow-page markets are getting wise to this and are trying to get the person to pay for the ad as well. If you want to use this idea, try contacting the phone company, not the yellow pages. Bob Kramer, of Kramer's Sew & Vac in Cincinnati, did the same thing. One of his competitors went out of business. Normally when you would call that number, you would get a message that it was disconnected. He paid the guy a hundred dollars for his permission for that message to announce a number change instead of a disconnect. The new number is Bob's!

This is one of those ideas that may not work every time, but it is certainly worth a shot. The worst that can happen is that they won't let you do it. But if it works, it can be a nice jump in your inbound calls.

In *Street Smart Marketing* we wrote about another very clever promotion involving the yellow pages. In a major western city there was a pizza chain that specialized in delivery. They were doing well and, of course, live and die by their yellow-page advertising. If you want a pizza delivered, in many cases people look up the ads in the yellow pages.

Then Domino's Pizza moved into the market. They had a large budget for advertising, including a full-page yellow-page ad with blue and red. This cost a fortune. This local chain had a much smaller ad and was pushed back about four pages from the front of the pizza section. Now, how can this little guy compete with Domino's? They certainly couldn't afford a larger ad, let alone a full page.

Well, the next year as soon as the new yellow pages came out, this small local chain ran a campaign that said, "Bring us the Domino's yellow-page ad from out of the phone book and you'll get 2-for-1 pizza!" People were ripping them out and bringing them in. You would be hard-pressed to find a Domino's yellow-page ad anywhere in this city.

Domino's was upset! They had to pay for that ad for the rest of the year.

Specialty Advertising: Toys or Tools?

You can spend a fortune on anything from imprinted coffee cups to calendars, clocks to calculators. It's my guess that most specialty advertising is a waste. You could probably find better use of those funds. But as long as the specialty item makes sense for you and helps you achieve a goal of some kind, you can consider it.

Is it important for your name and phone number to be in front of your client all the time? If not, then a specialty item only makes sense if it is being used as a gift around the holidays or as a special thank-you. For example, we stumbled onto an item that seems to be a big hit with our clients. We had custom polo shirts made with our

Streetfighting logo on it. The reason I had them done originally was that I wear this kind of shirt a lot and discovered that they cost about the same with a custom-made logo on them.

I started sending them to clients after a seminar or keynote speech as a thank-you, and we've gotten a tremendous response. We've sent other things out in the past, but never did we get the response from the clients as we have with this shirt.

This doesn't mean that everyone should go out and buy polo shirts. You need to think of something that your clients have need for or want anyway. Then provide it to them with your imprint.

Sometimes you can use a specialty item as an "excuse" to make a sales call and see the decision maker. It gives you a reason to visit and make contact. This technique is used by Edye Kaplan, a drug rep for a major pharmaceutical company. Their prescription drug logo was imprinted on boxes of microwave popcorn. When calling on doctors' offices, she was able to get in to see many doctors to deliver this gift. Often when she visits, the staff asks for more popcorn. It's a very inexpensive way to make impact.

George Walther, author of *Phone Power* and *Power Talking* and one of the nation's leading experts on use of the telephone, uses a twenty-five-foot red coil cord for his gift. It's also part of his logo. In his books, tapes, and seminars he recommends the use of a twenty-five-foot cord to give people using the phone freedom to move around. His logo is in the shape of a coil telephone cord. He doesn't need to have the cord imprinted (which would be difficult anyway). The cord *is* his logo. Does it work? We use one in our office. I was staring at his cord when writing this chapter. And now you know about his books, tapes, and seminars. I suppose it does work!

Advertising Agencies: Things You Should Know

In many of my seminars I'm asked the question of whether to use an advertising agency or not. It's a tough question to answer because the quality of agencies varies greatly. If you can find a good one that knows how to sell your product or service and is reasonable in their cost to you, they're probably worth their weight in gold. Unfortunately many are not.

Ad agencies get a 15 percent commission from the media. When you buy a $5,000 media schedule, the agency is billed 85 percent of that, or $4,250. The $750 is their commission for selling the media. In theory it should not cost any more to use an agency than to go direct, but in actuality it costs a lot more.

First, there is no agency commission paid by the daily newspaper. So if an agency buys newspaper space for you, they have to mark it up to make their 15 percent commission. On a $5,000 ad they'll bill you $5882.50. So it costs you more for a newspaper ad. Most clients don't want their agencies marking up newspaper, so agencies often stay away from newspaper advertising. If they don't mark up, they can't make any money at it. But what if newspaper is your best way to go?

To complicate the problem further, agencies can't make money at 15 percent. So they have to sell you expensive production, research, or other services to make a decent profit.

Another problem with many local agencies is that their creative people are often more interested in winning awards than getting sales for the client. Be careful. You can usually spot creative directors. They usually wear an unstructured linen jacket with the sleeves rolled up, untied Converse high-tops, and hair in a ponytail. If it's a woman, she'll carry a huge purse. You're not out to entertain the masses but rather to let your target audience know the benefits of working with you and to do it in a dignified way.

There seems to be a trend to work with agencies more on a fee basis. This would seem to make more sense. Pay your agency for their time and talent. Don't base it on the size of your advertising budget. This helps you to make sure that your goals and their goals are compatible. When working on a commission, the one way for an agency to make more money is to increase the advertising budget. But what if it's possible to get more results spending less money? You'll never know because there is no motivation to pursue that. The fee base compensation helps you move more toward that end.

Final Advertising Thoughts

These ideas are here as a starting point. There is no right or wrong answer. As a matter of fact, if you put three ad people in a room, you're likely to get five different opinions, unless there's a client present. There are approaches that break the rules and are tremendously successful. There are ads that seem to follow all the basics and totally bomb. Advertising is difficult. Part art, part science, and part common sense. You can drop a bundle very quickly. Trust your gut and your head.

Resource Guide

Note: For your convenience, you have been provided the phone numbers of the resources listed when available. These numbers are current as of this writing, but please understand that phone numbers often change. You may have to go through directory assistance for those numbers that have become out of service.

GMP: The Greatest Management Principle in the World, by Dr. Michael LeBoeuf. New York: Berkley Books. Teaches you how to get other people to do what you want them to do based on the principle: The things that get rewarded get done. Audio album available from Nightingale-Conant, 7300 N. Lehigh Ave., Chicago, IL 60648. (800) 323-5552; in Illinois (312) 647-0300. Video available from Coronet/ MTI Film & Video, Deerfield, IL. (800) 621-2131. Different programs available.

Great Brain Robbery, by Murray Raphel and Ray Considine. Book, self-published. Interesting stories and techniques for getting new customers. Fun to read and opens with some great examples of what we would call some super Streetfighters. Murray Raphel Advertising, Gordon's Alley, Atlantic City, NJ 08401. (609) 348-6646.

How to Get the Most out of Trade Shows, by Steve Miller. NTC Business Books. Available directly from the author: 33422 30th Ave. SW, Federal Way, WA 98027. (206) 874-9665; fax (206) 874-9666.

How to Win Customers and Keep Them for Life, by Dr. Michael LeBoeuf. New York: Berkley Books. The ultimate customer service book. Takes the concepts from *Greatest Management Principle* and applies them to keeping your customers happy. Audio available from Nightingale-Conant, 7300 N. Lehigh Ave., Chicago, IL 60648. (800) 323-5552; in Illinois (312) 647-0300. Video available from Cally Curtis Company, Hollywood, CA (purchase price $575, rental $130); can be ordered through the author, (504) 833-8873.

How to Work a Room: A Guide to Successfully Managing the Mingling, by Susan RoAne. Warner Books. The perfect book for learning how to network for client leads. The RoAne Group, 14 Wilder St., Ste. 100, San Francisco, CA 94131. (415) 239-2224.

Managing a Retail Staff to Success, by Harry Friedman. Audio or video, self-published. Once you get them in the front door, you have to buy or your advertising and marketing are wasted. This program helps you manage your sales staff. The Friedman Group, 8636 Sepulveda Blvd. Ste. C, Los Angeles, CA 90045. (800) 351-8040.

Managing the Future: 10 Driving Forces of Change for the '90s, by Robert B. Tucker. G. P. Putnam's Sons, New York: 1991.

Million Dollar Presentations (audio) replaces the *Million*

Dollar Close program by Bill Bishop. Some of the most effective sales and communications techniques found. Available directly from the author: Bill Bishop & Associates, 834 Gran Paseo Dr., Orlando, FL 32825. (407) 281-1395.

Mind Your Own Business, by Murray Raphel. Book, self-published. Murray Raphel Advertising, Gordon's Alley, Atlantic City, NJ 08401. (609) 348-6646.

Perfect Sales Presentation, by Robert L. Shook. New York: Bantam Books, 1987. Helps you learn sales from some of the nation's top salespeople.

Phone Power, by George Walther. Book can be ordered directly from the author: 401 Second Ave. S., Ste. 70, Seattle, WA 98104. (800) 843-8353; fax (206) 340-1160. Shows you how to get the most out of your phone. Also available on audio cassettes. Thirteen individual cassettes which can be ordered separately at $12.95 each or as a "Power Pack," which gets you the videotape free. The individual tapes cover different concepts including: Phone Power for the Person Who Manages, for Effective Communications, for the Receptionist, for the Switchboard Operator, for the Secretary, for the Outbound Telemarketer, for the Inbound Telemarketer, for Negotiation, for Dealing With Difficult People, for the Customer Service Professional, for the Salesperson, for Getting Appointments, for the Accounts Receivable Collector.

Power Speak, by Dorothy Leeds. New York: Prentice-Hall Press. Book, audio album (self-published), and video can be ordered from the author: Organizational Technologies, Inc., 800 West End Ave., Ste. 10A, New York, NY 10025. (212) 864-2424.

Power Talking: 50 Ways to Say What You Mean and Get What You Want, by George R. Walther. New York: G. P. Putnam's Sons, 1991.

Prime Prospects Unlimited (formally called *Gold Calling System*), by Bill Bishop. Audio, self-published. Six audiocassettes. This program is primarily for helping outside salespeople convert their cold calling to getting referred leads and setting up good qualified appointments, even over the phone. Available directly from the author: Bill Bishop & Associates, 834 Gran Paseo Dr., Orlando, FL 32825. (407) 281-1395.

Profitable Telemarketing: Total Training for Professional Excellence, by George Walther. Audio. Teaches you how to use the telephone to increase sales. Six cassette tapes. Nightingale-Conant Corporation. Can be ordered directly from the author: 401 Second Ave. S., Ste. 70, Seattle WA 98104. (800) 843-8353; fax (206) 340-1160.

Smart Questions, by Dorothy Leeds. New York: McGraw Hill. Book, audio album (self-published), and video can be ordered directly from the author: Organizational Technologies, Inc., 800 West End Ave., Ste. 10A, New York, NY 10025. (212) 864-2424.

Stalls Are for Horses, Not Sales People, video by Bill Bishop. Audio, self-published. Ten techniques for getting people to make a decision and get off of dead center. Helpful in working with customers or store managers. When conducting field consulting. Two-hour video tape. Available directly from the author: Bill Bishop & Associates, 834 Gran Paseo Dr., Orlando, FL 32825. (407) 281-1395.

Streetfighter's Neighborhood Sales Builders, by Jeff Slutsky. Recorded live at a full-day seminar, teaches you step by step the complete Streetfighting program. It comes with the *Streetfighter's Workbook* which becomes your customized plan of attack. $150 or less as part of the "Streetfighter's Profit Package." Six tapes/100-page workbook. Streetfighter

Marketing, 467 Waterbury Ct., Gahanna, OH 43230. (614) 337-7474.

Streetfighter's Profit Package, by Jeff Slutsky. Package contains one-hour VHS. The complete six-cassette Neighborhood Sales Builders audio album with workbook, *Streetfighting: Low Cost Advertising/Promotion for Your Business* and *Street Smart Marketing,* $299.95, or $349.95 with *The 33 Secrets of Street Smart Tele-Selling* cassette album and workbook. Add $3.50 shipping and handling. Order from Streetfighter Marketing, 467 Waterbury Ct., Gahanna, OH 43230. (614) 337-7474; (800) 837-7355 (SELL); fax (614) 337-2233.

Streetfighting: Low Cost Advertising/Promotions for Your Business, by Jeff Slutsky. This book was the predecessor to *Street Smart Marketing.* You will find more anecdotes and examples of successful promotions plus four complete chapters geared to getting the most from your radio, TV, outdoor, and print advertising. $29.95 or less as part of complete audio and video "Profit Package." Available directly from the author: Streetfighter Marketing, 467 Waterbury Ct., Gahanna, OH 43230. (614) 337-7474.

Successful Retail Selling, by Harry Friedman. Audio or video, self-published. Techniques for getting the customer to buy once they are already in your store. The Friedman Group, 8636 Sepulveda Blvd., Ste. C, Los Angeles, CA 90045. (800) 351-8040.

Successful Telephone Selling in the 90's, by Martin D. Shafiroff and Robert L. Shook. Techniques for selling by telephone. New York: HarperCollins, 1990.

33 Secrets of Street Smart Tele-Selling Workbook, by Jeff and Marc Slutsky. Teaches you a Streetfighter's approach to telemarketing. Available directly from the author: Retail Marketing Institute, 467 Waterbury Ct., Gahanna, OH

43230. (614) 337-7474. $19.95 individually or is included as part of the audiocassette album (Prentice-Hall, $70) or for less as part of the "Profit Package Plus" audio/video program.

33 Secrets of Street Smart Tele-Selling, by Jeff and Marc Slutsky. Englewood Cliffs, N.J.: Prentice-Hall. Provides you a streetfighter's approach to telephone selling techniques. $70. 3 tapes/workbook and book available from author: (614) 337-7474.

Word-of-Mouth Marketing, by Jerry R. Wilson. New York: John Wiley & Sons, 1991. Available also through the author: (800) 428-5666 or (317) 257-6876.

Working Smart, by Dr. Michael LeBoeuf. New York: Warner Books, 1979. Time management and goal-setting techniques. *Working Smarter* available in audio from Nightingale-Conant.

TACTICAL TOOLS AND OTHER RESOURCES

The resources suggested here are done so for your convenience and to help you develop and implement your Streetfighting program as effectively and efficiently as possible. In some cases we were provided samples to use and review but other than that we receive no payments, royalties, or commission. These are suggested because we feel your program will be enhanced by their use.

Annual Planning Wall Calendar. Our favorite is the Smart Chart, by John Lee Companies, P.O. Box 398R, Crawfordsville, FL 32327. (904) 926-7122. They also provide some very helpful hints on using this calendar most effectively.

Archer Telephone Recorder. Allows you to record your

own telephone conversations. Plugs into any cassette recorder with a remote plug. Starts recording when you pick up the handset and stops when you hang up. Available at any Radio Shack store. Great for helping you review and improve your tele-consulting or teleselling skills.

Comlink. Device that allows your computer modem (using TeleMagic) to dial directly through most phone systems. (800) 869-1420.

Duophone Computerized Phone Accountant. Tracks all the incoming and outgoing calls on calculator tape. Tells you length of each call, time, date, and codes calls. If you are doing a lot of calling, this can be real helpful. Not necessary if you use TeleMagic. Good only on one line at a time (unless you get more units). Available at any Radio Shack. About $100.

Headsets of professional quality. Allows for hands-free operations. Especially good for field marketing people who need to contact numerous neighborhood-level managers during the development and implementation phase of a neighborhood marketing program. Some retail operations using teleselling techniques will also find this very useful. Must use professional-quality headsets. Recommended vendor: Plantronics, 345 Encinal St., Santa Cruz, CA 95060. (800) 538-0748; in California (800) 662-3902.

Index Card Filing System. Available through Caddylak Systems, Inc., 131 Heartland Blvd., P.O. Box W, Brentwood, NY 11717-0698. (800) 523-8060; (516) 254-2000; fax (516) 254-2018. Thirty-day money-back guarantee offered when item is returned in original carton. Catalog available.

King T-UT TeleMagic Utility Program. Item #470000. Business Systems Consultants. 2675 W. Highway 89A, #401, Sedona, AZ 86336. (602) 282-9070.

Laplink III. Allows your laptop computer to share information with your desktop without diskettes. Available from Traveling Software, Inc., 18702 N. Creek Pky., Bothell, WA 98011. (800) 662-2652; (206) 483-8088.

Lynx System Status Card Holder. Available through Remarkable Products, 245 Pegasus Ave., Northvale, NJ 07647. (201) 784-0900; fax (201) 767-7463. Comes with five colors of T cards. Catalog available.

Novell Netware Local Area Network (LAN). Allows all of your computers to share information and printers as well as numerous other functions. Very important when using TeleMagic on more than one computer. (800) 453-1267.

TeleMagic Telemarketing Computer Software, written by Michael McCafferty. Computer software for single user or network telemarketing program. Available for PC and Macintosh. Suggested machine requires 640K RAM, 20 meg hard drive, modem. Can work on two diskette drives and 512K RAM. Published by Remote Control Computer Support Group, 514 Via de la Valle, Ste. 306, Solana Beach, CA 92075. (800) 992-9952; (619) 481-8577.

Other Books and Tapes by the Brothers Slutsky

Streetfighting: Low Cost Advertising/Promotion for Your Business
Street Smart Marketing
Street Smart Tele-Selling: The 33 Secrets
Streetfighter's Neighborhood Sales Builders
Confessions of a Streetfighter